Nathaniel Cotton

Various Pieces in Verse and Prose

In Two Volumes. Vol. I

Nathaniel Cotton

Various Pieces in Verse and Prose
In Two Volumes. Vol. I

ISBN/EAN: 9783744689212

Printed in Europe, USA, Canada, Australia, Japan

Cover: Foto ©Thomas Meinert / pixelio.de

More available books at **www.hansebooks.com**

VARIOUS PIECES

IN

VERSE AND PROSE.

BY THE LATE

NATHANIEL COTTON, M.D.

MANY OF WHICH WERE NEVER BEFORE PUBLISHED.

Vitæ fanctitas fumma, comitas par. Infectatur vitia, non homines.   PLIN. EP. x.

Edendum autem ex pluribus caufis—maximè quòd libelli, quos emifit, dicuntur in manibus effe, quamvis jam gratiam novitatis exuerint.   PLIN. EP. ii.

IN TWO VOLUMES.

VOL. I.

TO THE

DOWAGER COUNTESS

SPENCER,

THESE TWO SMALL VOLUMES

ARE, BY PERMISSION,

INSCRIBED.

THE Author being well known to her Ladyſhip for many years, this public teſtimony of approbation of his Life and Works given by her, whoſe high ſtation and rank preclude her not from a laudable and eminent zeal in the cauſe of religion and goodneſs, is particularly acknowledged by

Her Ladyship's

Moſt obliged,

And moſt obedient ſervant,

NATH^L. COTTON.

THE PREFACE.

AS the VISIONS IN VERSE, and other Pieces of the late Dr. COTTON, which have made their appearance, have given general satisfaction, the Editor flatters himself that the present volumes, some pieces in which have not yet been published, will be acceptable to the Public.

It may not be improper to observe, in regard to the SERMONS here offered, that as Mr. Boyle, Mr. Locke, Sir Isaac Newton, and Mr. Addison,

Addison, were firm believers in Christianity; that being *laymen*, and having no temporal *interests* relative to religion, their influence in the support of it has been extensive and effectual: So every fresh instance of a firm faith, in a mind far removed from all suspicion, will be acceptable to the lovers of Christianity.

CONTENTS

TO

VOLUME I.

FABLES.   Page.
   I. The Bee, the Ant, and the Sparrow — 1
  II. The Scholar and the Cat — — 8
 III. Neptune and the Mariners — — 13
 IV. The Beau and the Viper — — 17
  V. The Snail and the Gardener — — 22
 VI. The Farmer and the Horse — — 28

TALES, &c.   —   —   —   38—51

EPITAPHS   —   —   —   52—55

VARIOUS PIECES.
  An Invocation of Happiness — — 56
  Time and Chance — — — 58
  An Enigma, inscribed to Miss P. — — 62
  The Fire Side — — — 65
  To some Children listening to a Lark — 69
  To a Child of five years old — — 71
  On Lord Cobham's Garden — — 72

To-morrow

CONTENTS.

To-morrow	72
Allusion to Horace, Ode XVI. Book II.	74
Epitaph on Mr. Thomas Strong	82
Epitaph upon Miss Gee	82
Rebusses	83, 84, 85
Some hasty Rhymes on Sleep	86
Rebus on Miss James	88
A Song	88
A Sunday Hymn	89
Ode on the Messiah	90
Ode on the New Year	94
Epitaph on John Duke of Bridgwater	96
A Fable	97
Addressed to a young Lady	104

RIDDLES — 106—112

Psalm XIII.	113
——— XLII.	114
The Night Piece	117
To the Rev. James Hervey, on his Meditations	122
Lines under a Sun Dial	125
To the Memory of the Rev. Samuel Clarke	126

VISIONS IN VERSE — 129

FABLES.

FABLES.

The Advantages of Application and Diligence in our earlier Years, and the destructive Consequences of Pride and Cruelty.

FABLE I.

The BEE, *the* ANT, *and the* SPARROW.

MY dears, 'tis said in days of old,
That beasts could talk, and birds could scold.
But now it seems the human race
Alone engross the speaker's place.
Yet lately, if report be true,
(And much the tale relates to you)
There met a Sparrow, Ant, and Bee,
Which reason'd and convers'd as we.

FABLE I.

Who reads my page will doubtless grant,
That Phe's the wife induſtrious Ant.
And all with half an eye may ſee,
That Kitty is the buſy Bee.
Here then are two—But where's the third?
Go ſearch your ſchool, you'll find the Bird.
Your ſchool! I aſk your pardon, Fair,
I'm ſure you'll find no Sparrow there.

   Now to my tale.—One ſummer's morn
A Bee rang'd o'er the verdant lawn;
Studious to huſband every hour,
And make the moſt of every flow'r.
Nimble from ſtalk to ſtalk ſhe flies,
And loads with yellow wax her thighs;
With which the artiſt builds her comb,
And keeps all tight and warm at home;
Or from the cowſlip's golden bells
Sucks honey to enrich her cells;
Or every tempting roſe purſues,
Or ſips the lily's fragrant dews,
Yet never robs the ſhining bloom,
Or of its beauty, or perfume.

                                          Thus

FABLE I.

Thus she discharg'd in every way,
The various duties of the day.

It chanc'd a frugal Ant was near,
Whose brow was furrow'd o'er by care:
A great œconomist was she,
Nor less laborious than the Bee;
By pensive parents often taught
What ills arise from want of thought;
That poverty on sloth depends,
On poverty the loss of friends.
Hence every day the Ant is found
With anxious steps to tread the ground;
With curious search to trace the grain,
And drag the heavy load with pain.

The active Bee with pleasure saw
The Ant fulfil her parents law.
Ah! sister-labourer, says she,
How very fortunate are we!
Who taught in infancy to know,
The comforts which from labour flow,
Are independent of the Great,
Nor know the wants of pride and state.

FABLE I.

Who reads my page will doubtless grant,
That Phe's the wife industrious Ant.
And all with half an eye may see,
That Kitty is the busy Bee.
Here then are two—But where's the third?
Go search your school, you'll find the Bird.
Your school! I ask your pardon, Fair,
I'm sure you'll find no Sparrow there.

Now to my tale.—One summer's morn
A Bee rang'd o'er the verdant lawn;
Studious to husband every hour,
And make the most of every flow'r.
Nimble from stalk to stalk she flies,
And loads with yellow wax her thighs;
With which the artist builds her comb,
And keeps all tight and warm at home;
Or from the cowslip's golden bells
Sucks honey to enrich her cells;
Or every tempting rose pursues,
Or sips the lily's fragrant dews,
Yet never robs the shining bloom,
Or of its beauty, or perfume.

Thus

FABLE I.

Thus she discharg'd in every way,
The various duties of the day.

It chanc'd a frugal Ant was near,
Whose brow was furrow'd o'er by care:
A great œconomist was she,
Nor less laborious than the Bee;
By pensive parents often taught
What ills arise from want of thought;
That poverty on sloth depends,
On poverty the loss of friends.
Hence every day the Ant is found
With anxious steps to tread the ground;
With curious search to trace the grain,
And drag the heavy load with pain.

The active Bee with pleasure saw
The Ant fulfil her parents law.
Ah! sister-labourer, says she,
How very fortunate are we!
Who taught in infancy to know,
The comforts which from labour flow,
Are independent of the Great,
Nor know the wants of pride and state.

FABLE I.

Why is our food so very sweet?
Because we earn before we eat.
Why are our wants so very few?
Because we Nature's calls pursue.
Whence our complacency of mind?
Because we act our parts assign'd.
Have we incessant tasks to do?
Is not all Nature busy too?
Doth not the sun with constant pace
Persist to run his annual race?
Do not the stars which shine so bright,
Renew their courses every night?
Doth not the ox obedient bow
His patient neck, and draw the plow?
Or when did e'er the generous steed
Withhold his labour or his speed?
If you all Nature's system scan,
The only idle thing is Man.

A wanton Sparrow long'd to hear
This sage discourse, and strait drew near.
The Bird was talkative and loud,
And very pert, and very proud;

FABLE I.

As worthless and as vain a thing
Perhaps as ever wore a wing.
She found, as on a spray she sat,
The little friends were deep in chat;
That virtue was their favourite theme,
And toil and probity their scheme:
Such talk was hateful to her breast,
She thought them arrant prudes at best.
When to display her naughty mind,
Hunger with cruelty combin'd;
She view'd the ant with savage eyes,
And hopt, and hopt to snatch her prize.
The Bee, who watch'd her opening bill,
And guess'd her fell design to kill;
Ask'd her from what her anger rose,
And why she treated Ants as foes?

 The Sparrow her reply began,
And thus the conversation ran.

 Whenever I'm dispos'd to dine,
I think the whole creation mine;
That I'm a bird of high degree,
And every insect made for me.

FABLE I.

Hence oft I search the Emmet brood,
For Emmets are delicious food.
And oft in wantonness and play,
I slay ten thousand in a day:
For truth it is, without disguise,
That I love mischief as my eyes.

  Oh! fie, the honest Bee reply'd,
I fear you make base man your guide.
Of every creature sure the worst,
Tho' in creation's scale the first!
Ungrateful man! 'tis strange he thrives,
Who burns the Bees to rob their hives!
I hate his vile administration,
And so do all the Emmet nation.
What fatal foes to birds are men,
Quite from the eagle to the wren!
Oh! do not men's example take,
Who mischief do for mischief's sake;
But spare the Ant—her worth demands
Esteem and friendship at your hands.
A mind, with every virtue blest,
Must raise compassion in your breast.

                        Virtue!

FABLE I.

Virtue! rejoin'd the sneering bird,
Where did you learn that gothick word?
Since I was hatch'd I never heard
That virtue was at all rever'd.
But say it was the antients' claim,
Yet moderns disavow the name.
Unless, my dear, you read romances,
I cannot reconcile your fancies.
Virtue in fairy tales is seen
To play the goddess, or the queen;
But what's a queen without the pow'r,
Or beauty, child, without a dow'r?
Yet this is all that virtue brags;
At best 'tis only worth in rags.
Such whims my very heart derides,
Indeed you make me burst my sides.
Trust me, Miss Bee—to speak the truth,
I've copied man from earliest youth;
The same our taste, the same our school,
Passion and appetite our rule;
And call me Bird, or call me sinner,
I'll ne'er forego my sport or dinner.

A prowling Cat the miscreant spies,
And wide expands her amber eyes.
Near and more near Grimalkin draws,
She wags her tail, protends her paws;
Then springing on her thoughtless prey,
She bore the vicious bird away.
   Thus in her cruelty and pride,
The wicked, wanton Sparrow dy'd.

That true Virtue consists in Action, and not in Speculation.

FABLE II.
The SCHOLAR and the CAT.

LABOUR entitles man to eat,
   The idle have no claim to meat.
This rule must every station fit,
Because 'tis drawn from sacred writ.
And yet, to feed on such condition,
Almost amounts to prohibition.
Rome's priesthood wou'd be doom'd, I fear,
To eat soup maigre all the year.

                                 And

FABLE II.

And wou'd not Oxford's cloister'd son
By this hard statute be undone?
In truth, your poet, were he fed
No oft'ner than he earns his bread,
The vengeance of this law wou'd feel,
And often go without a meal.

 It seem'd a Scholar and his Cat
Together join'd in social chat.
When thus the letter'd youth began—
Of what vast consequence is man!
Lords of this nether globe we shine,
Our tenure's held by right divine.
Here independence waves its plea,
All creatures bow the vassal knee.
Nor earth alone can bound our reign,
Ours is the empire of the main.

 True—man's a sovereign prince—but say,
What art sustains the monarch's sway.
Say from what source we fetch supplies,
'Tis here the grand enquiry lies.
Strength is not man's—for strength must suit
Best with the structure of a brute.

Nor

Nor craft nor cunning can suffice,
A fox might then dispute the prize.
To God-like Reason 'tis we owe
Our ball and sceptre here below.

   Now your associate next explains
To whom precedence appertains.
And sure 'tis easy to divine
The leaders of this royal line.
Note that all tradesmen I attest
But petty princes at the best.
Superior excellence you'll find
In those, who cultivate the mind.
Hence heads of colleges, you'll own,
Transcend th' assessors of a throne.
Say, Evans, have you any doubt?
You can't offend by speaking out.

   With visage placid and sedate,
Puss thus address'd her learned mate.

   We're told that none in Nature's plan
Disputes pre-eminence with man.
But this is still a dubious case
To me, and all our purring race.

We

FABLE II.

We grant indeed to partial eyes
Men may appear fupremely wife.
But our fagacious rabbies hold,
That all which glitters is not gold.
Pray, if your haughty claims be true,
Why are our manners ap'd by you?
Whene'er you think, all Cats agree,
You fhut your optics, juft as we.
Pray, why like Cats fo wrapt in thought,
If you by Cats were never taught?
But know, our tabby fchools maintain
Worth is not center'd in the brain.
Not that our fages thought defpife—
No—but in action virtue lies.
We find it by experience fact,
That thought muft ripen into act;
Or Cat no real fame acquires,
But virtue in the bud expires.
This point your orchard can decide—
Obferve its gay autumnal pride.
For trees are held in high repute,
Not for their bloffoms, but their fruit.

If

If fo, then Millar's page decrees
Mere Scholars to be barren trees.
But if thefe various reafons fail,
Let my example once prevail.

 When to your chamber you repair,
Your property employs my care.
And while you fink in fweet repofe,
My faithful eyelids never clofe.
When hunger prompts the moufe to fteal,
Then I difplay my honeft zeal;
True to my charge, thefe talons feize
The wretch, who dares purloin your cheefe.
Or fhould the thief affault your bread,
I ftrike the audacious felon dead.

 Nor fay I fpring at fmaller game—
My prowefs flaughter'd rats proclaim.
I'm told, your generals often fly,
When danger, and when death are nigh.
Nay, when nor death nor danger's near,
As your court-martials make appear.
When in your fervice we engage,
We brave the pilfering villain's rage;

Ne'er

FABLE III.

Ne'er take advantage of the night,
To meditate inglorious flight;
But stand resolv'd, when foes defy,
To conquer, or to bravely die.
  Hence, Bookworm, learn our duty here
Is active life in every sphere.
Know too, there's scarce a brute but can
Instruct vain supercilious man.

―――――――

That our Fortitude and Perseverance should be proportionate to the Degree and Duration of our Sufferings.

FABLE III.
NEPTUNE *and the* MARINERS.

WHEN sore calamities we feel,
  And sorrow treads on sorrow's heel,
Our courage and our strength, we say,
Are insufficient for the day.
'Thus man's a poor dejected elf,
Who fain would run away from self.

Yet

FABLE III.

Yet turn to Germany, you'll find
An Atlas of a human mind!
But here I deviate from my plan,
For Pruſſia's king is more than man!
Inferior beings ſuit my rhime,
My ſcheme, my genius, and my time;
Men, birds, and beaſts, with now and then
A pagan god, to grace my pen.

A veſſel bound for India's coaſt,
The merchants confidence and boaſt,
Puts forth to ſea—the gentle deep
Beſpeaks its boiſterous god aſleep.
Three chearful ſhouts the ſailors gave,
And zephyrs curl the ſhining wave.
A halcyon ſky prevails awhile,
The tritons and the nereids ſmile.
Theſe omens faireſt hopes impreſs,
And half inſure the George ſucceſs.

What caſual ills theſe hopes deſtroy!
To change how ſubject every joy!
When dangers moſt remote appear,
Experience proves thoſe dangers near.

FABLE III.

Thus, boast of health whene'er you please,
Health is next neighbour to disease.
'Tis prudence to suspect a foe,
And fortitude to meet the blow.
In wisdom's rank he stands the first,
Who stands prepar'd to meet the worst.

   For lo! unnumber'd clouds arise,
The sable legions spread the skies.
The storm around the vessel raves,
The deep displays a thousand graves.
With active hands and fearless hearts
The sailors play their various parts;
They ply the pumps, they furl the sails,
Yet nought their diligence avails.
The tempest thickens every hour,
And mocks the feats of human pow'r.

   The sailors now their fate deplore,
Estrang'd to every fear before.
With wild surprise their eye-balls glare,
Their honest breasts admit despair.
All further efforts they decline,
At once all future hopes resign;

                          And

FABLE III.

And thus abandoning their skill,
They give the ship to drive at will.
   Strait enter'd with majestic grace,
A form of more than human race,
The god an azure mantle wore,
His hand a forked sceptre bore;
When thus the monarch of the main—
   How dare you deem your labours vain?
Shall man exert himself the less,
Because superior dangers press?
How can I think your hearts sincere,
Unless you bravely persevere?
Know, mortals, that when perils rise,
Perils enhance the glorious prize.
But, who deserts himself, shall be
Deserted by the gods and me.
Hence to your charge, and do your best,
My trident shall do all the rest.
   The mariners their task renew,
All to their destin'd province flew.
The winds are hush'd—the sea subsides,
The gallant George in safety rides.

The Folly of passing a hasty and derogatory Judgment upon the noxious Animals of the Creation.

FABLE IV.

The BEAU *and the* VIPER.

ALL wise philosophers maintain
Nature created nought in vain.
Yet some with supercilious brow,
Deny the truth asserted now.
What if I shew that only man,
Appears defective in the plan!
Say, will the sceptic lay aside
His sneers, his arrogance, and pride?

   A Beau, imported fresh from France,
Whose study was to dress and dance;
Who had betimes, in Gallia's school,
Grafted the coxcomb on the fool;
Approach'd a wood one summer's day,
To screen him from the scorching ray,
And as he travers'd thro' the grove,
Scheming of gallantry and love,

A Viper's

FABLE IV.

A Viper's spiry folds were seen,
Sparkling with azure, gold, and green;
The Beau indignant, weak, and proud,
With transport thus exclaim'd aloud:—
 Avaunt, detested fiend of night!
Thou torture to the human sight!
To every reptile a disgrace,
And fatal to our god-like race.
Why were such creatures form'd as you,
Unless to prove my doctrine true;
That when we view this nether sphere,
Nor wisdom nor design appear?
 The Serpent rais'd his angry crest,
An honest zeal inflam'd his breast.
His hissings struck the fopling's ear,
And shook his very soul with fear.
Inglorious wretch! the Viper cries,
How dare you broach infernal lies?
Is there, in all creation's chain,
A link so worthless and so vain?
Grant that your dress were truly thine,
How can your gold compare with mine?

FABLE IV.

Your vestments are of garter hue,
Mine boast a far superior blue.

You style me Reptile in contempt,
You are that very reptile meant;
A two-legg'd thing which crawls on earth,
Void of utility and worth.

You call me fatal to your race—
Was ever charge so false and base?
You can't in all your annals find,
That unprovok'd we hurt mankind.
Uninjur'd men in mischief deal,
We only bite the hostile heel.

Do not we yield our lives to feed,
And save your vile distemper'd breed?
When leprosy pollutes your veins,
Do not we purge the loathsome stains?
When riot and excess prevail,
And health, and strength, and spirits fail;
Doctors from us their aid derive,
Hence penitential rakes revive.
We bleed to make the caitiffs dine, *
Or drown to medicate their wine.

---

* Upon some occasions Vipers are dressed, and served to table as eels.

You aſk, my poiſon to what end?
Minute philoſopher, attend.
  Nature, munificent and wiſe,
To all our wants adapts ſupplies.
Our frames are fitted to our need,
Hence greyhounds are endu'd with ſpeed.
Lions by force their prey ſubdue,
By force maintain their empire too:
But power, altho' the lion's fame,
Was never known the Viper's claim.
Obſerve, when I unroll my length—
Say, is my ſtructure form'd for ſtrength?
Doth not celerity imply
Or legs to run, or wings to fly?
My jaws are conſtituted weak,
Hence poiſon lurks behind my cheek.
As lightning quick my fangs convey
This liquid to my wounded prey.
The venom thus infures my bite,
For wounds preclude the victim's flight.
  But why this deadly juice, you cry,
To make the wretched captive die?

FABLE IV.

Why not possess'd of stronger jaws,
Or arm'd like savage brutes with claws?
   Can such weak arguments persuade?
Ask rather, why were Vipers made?
To me my poison's more than wealth,
And to ungrateful mortals health.
In this benevolent design
My various organs all combine.
Strike out the poison from my frame,
My system were no more the same.
I then should want my comforts due,
Nay, lose my very being too.
And you'd, as doctors all agree,
A sovereign medicine lose in me.
   Now learn, 'tis arrogance in man,
To censure what he cannot scan.
Nor dare to charge God's works with ill,
Since Vipers kind designs fulfil:
But give injurious scruples o'er,
Be still, be humble, and adore.

That Happiness is much more equally distributed, than the Generality of Mankind are apprized of.

FABLE V.
The Snail and the Gardener.

WHEN sons of fortune ride on high,
How do we point the admiring eye!
With foolish face of wonder gaze,
And often covet what we praise.
How do we partial Nature chide,
As deaf to every son beside!
Or censure the mistaken dame,
As if her optics were to blame!
Thus we deem Nature most unkind,
Or what's as bad, we deem her blind.
But when inferior ranks we see,
Who move in humbler spheres than we;
Men by comparisons are taught,
Nature is not so much in fault.
Yet mark my tale—the poet's pen
Shall vindicate her ways to men.

Within

FABLE V.

Within a garden, far from town,
There dwelt a Snail of high renown;
Who, by tradition as appears,
Had been a tenant several years.
She spent her youth in wisdom's page—
Hence honour'd and rever'd in age.
Do Snails at any time contend,
Insult a neighbour, or a friend;
Dispute their property, and share,
Or in a cherry, or a pear?
No lord chief justice, all agree,
So able, and so just as she!
Whichever way their causes went,
All parties came away content.
At length she found herself decay,
Death sent mementos every day.
Her drooping strength sustains no more
The shell, which on her back she bore.
The eye had lost its visual art,
The heavy ear refus'd its part;
The teeth perform'd their office ill,
And every member fail'd her will.

But no defects in mind appear,
Her intellects are strong and clear.
Thus when his glorious course is run,
How brightly shines the setting sun!

The news thro' all the garden spread,
The neighbours throng'd about her bed;
Chearful she rais'd her voice aloud,
And thus addres'd the weeping crowd.

My friends, I'm hast'ning to the grave,
And know, nor plum, nor peach can save.
Yes, to those mansions go I must,
Where our good fathers sleep in dust.
Nor am I backward to explore
That gloomy vale they trod before.
'Gainst fate's decree what can I say?
Like other Snails I've had my day.
Full many summer suns I've seen,
And now die grateful and serene.

If men the higher pow'rs arraign,
Shall we adopt the plaintive strain?
Nature, profuse to us and ours,
Hath kindly built these stately tow'rs;

Where,

FABLE V.

Where, when the skies in night are drest,
Secure from every ill we rest.
Survey our curious structure well—
How firm, and yet how light our shell!
Our refuge, when cold storms invade,
And in the dog-days' heat our shade.

   Thus when we see a fleeter race,
We'll not lament our languid pace.
Do dangers rise, or foes withstand?
Are not our castles close at hand?
For let a Snail at distance roam,
The happy Snail is still at home.

   Survey our gardens blest retreats—
Oh! what a paradise of sweets!
With what variety it's stor'd!
Unnumber'd dainties spread our board.
The plums assume their glossy blue,
And cheeks of nectarines glow for you;
Peaches their lovely blush betray,
And apricots their gold display;
While for your beverage, when you dine,
There streams the nectar of the vine.

Be not my dying words forgot;
Depart, contented with your lot;
Repress complaints when they begin,
Ingratitude's a crying sin.
And hold it for a truth, that we
Are quite as blest as Snails should be.

The Gardener hears with great surprise
This sage discourse, and thus he cries—
Oh! what a thankless wretch am I,
Who pass ten thousand favours by!
I blame, whene'er the linnet sings,
My want of song, or want of wings.
The piercing hawk, with towering flight,
Reminds me of deficient sight.
And when the generous steed I view,
Is not his strength my envy too?
I thus at birds and beasts repine,
And wish their various talents mine.
Fool as I am, who cannot see
Reason is more than all to me.

My landlord boasts a large estate,
Rides in his coach, and eats in plate.

What!

FABLE V.

What! shall these lures bewitch my eye?
Shall they extort the murmuring sigh?
Say, he enjoys superior wealth—
Is not my better portion, health?
Before the sun has gilt the skies,
Returning labour bids me rise;
Obedient to the hunter's horn,
He quits his couch at early morn.
By want compell'd, I dig the soil,
His is a voluntary toil.
For truth it is, since Adam's fall,
His sons must labour, one and all.
No man's exempted by his purse,
Kings are included in the curse.
Wou'd monarchs relish what they eat?
'Tis toil that makes the manchet sweet;
Nature enacts, before they're fed,
That prince and peasant earn their bread.
    Hence wisdom and experience show,
That bliss in equal currents flow;
That happiness is still the same,
How'er ingredients change their name.

Nor doth this theme our search defy,
'Tis level to the human eye.
Distinctions, introduc'd by men,
Bewilder, and obscure our ken.
I'll store these lessons in my heart,
And chearful act my proper part.
If sorrows rise, as sorrows will,
I'll stand resign'd to every ill;
Convinc'd, that wisely every pack
Is suited to the bearer's back.

That the Complaints of Mankind, against their several Stations and Provinces in Life, are often frivolous, and always unwarrantable.

FABLE VI.

The FARMER and the HORSE.

" 'TIS a vain world, and all things show it,
" I thought so once, but now I know it *."
Ah! GAY! is thy poetic page
The child of disappointed age?

* Gay's Epitaph.

FABLE VI.

Talk not of threescore years and ten,
For what avails our knowledge then?
   But grant, that this experienc'd truth
Were ascertain'd in early youth;
Reader, what benefit would flow?
I vow, I'm at a loss to know.
The world alarms the human breast,
Because in savage colours drest.
'Tis treated with invective style,
And stands impeach'd of fraud and guile.
All in this heavy charge agree—
But who's in fault—the world, or we?
The question's serious, short, and clear,
The answer claims our patient ear.
Yet if this office you decline—
With all my heart—the task be mine.
I'm certain, if I do my best,
Your candour will excuse the rest.
   A Farmer, with a pensive brow,
One morn accompany'd his plow.
The larks their chearful matins sung,
The woods with answering music rung;

The

FABLE VI.

The sun display'd his golden ray,
And Nature hail'd the rising day.
But still the peasant all the while
Refus'd to join the general smile.
He, like his fathers long before,
Resembled much the Jews of yore;
Whose murmurs impious, weak, and vain,
Nor quails nor manna could restrain.
   Did accidental dearth prevail?
How prone to tell his piteous tale!
Pregnant with joys did plenty rise?
How prone to blame indulgent skies!
Thus ever ready to complain,
For plenty sinks the price of grain.
   At length he spake:—Ye powers divine,
Was ever lot so hard as mine?
From infant life an arrant slave,
Close to the confines of the grave.
Have not I follow'd my employ
Near threescore winters, man and boy?
But since I call'd this farm my own,
What scenes of sorrow have I known!

FABLE VI.

Alas! if all the truth were told,
Hath not the rot impair'd my fold?
Hath not the meafles feiz'd my fwine?
Hath not the murrain flain my kine?
Or fay that horfes be my theme,
Hath not the ftaggers thinn'd my team?
Have not a thoufand ills befide
Depriv'd my ftable of its pride?

When I furvey my lands around,
What thorns and thiftles fpread my ground!
Doth not the grain my hopes beguile,
And mildews mock the threfher's toil?
However poor the harvefts paft,
What fo deficient as the laft!
But tho' nor blafts, nor mildews rife,
My turnips are deftroy'd by flies;
My fheep are pin'd to fuch degree,
That not a butcher comes to me.

Seafons are chang'd from what they were,
And hence too foul, or hence too fair.
Now fcorching heat and drought annoy,
And now returning fhowers deftroy.

Thus

FABLE VI.

Thus have I pafs'd my better years
'Midſt difappointments, cares, and tears.
And now, when I compute my gains,
What have I reap'd for all my pains?

Oh! had I known in manhood's prime
Thefe flow convictions wrought by time;
Would I have brav'd the various woes
Of fummer funs, and winter fnows?
Would I have tempted every fky,
So wet, fo windy, or fo dry?
With all the elements at ftrife?
Ah! no—I then had plann'd a life,
Where wealth attends the middle ftage,
And reft and comfort wait on age.
Where rot and murrain ne'er commence,
Nor paftures burn at my expence;
Nor injur'd cows their wants bewail,
Nor dairies mourn the milklefs pail;
Nor barns lament the blafted grain,
Nor cattle curfe the barren plain.

Dun hobbled by his mafter's fide,
And thus the fober brute reply'd:—

FABLE VI.

Look thro' your team, and where's the steed
Who dares dispute with me his breed?
Few horses trace their lineage higher,
Godolphin's Arab was my sire;
My dam was sprung from Panton's stud,
My grandam boasted Childers' blood.
But ah! it now avails me not
By what illustrious chief begot!
Spavins pay no regard to birth,
And failing vision sinks my worth.
The Squire, when he disgusted grew,
Transferr'd his property to you.
And since poor Dun " became your own,
" What scenes of sorrow have I known!"
Hath it not been my constant toil
To drag the plow, and turn the soil?
Are not my bleeding shoulders wrung
By large and weighty loads of dung?
When the shorn meadows claim your care,
And fragrant cocks perfume the air;
When Ceres' ripen'd fruits abound,
And Plenty waves her sheaves around;

True to my collar, home I bear
The treasures of the fruitful year.
And tho' this drudgery be mine,
You never heard me once repine.

Yet what rewards have crown'd my days?
I'm grudg'd the poor reward of praise.
For oats small gratitude I owe,
Beans were untasted joys, you know.
And now I'm hast'ning to my end,
Past services can find no friend.
Infirmities, disease, and age,
Provoke my surly driver's rage.
Look to my wounded flanks, you'll see
No horse was ever us'd like me.

But now I eat my meals with pain,
Averse to masticate the grain.
Hence you direct, at night and morn,
That chaff accompany my corn;
For husks, altho' my teeth be few,
Force my reluctant jaws to chew.
What then? of life shall I complain,
And call it fleeting, false, and vain?

FABLE VI.

Against the world shall I inveigh,
Because my grinders now decay?
   You think it were the wiser plan,
Had I consorted ne'er with man;
Had I my liberty maintain'd,
Or liberty by flight regain'd,
And rang'd o'er distant hills and dales
With the wild foresters of Wales.
   Grant I succeeded to my mind—
Is happiness to hills confin'd?
Don't famine oft erect her throne
Upon the rugged mountain's stone?
And don't the lower pastures fail,
When snows descending choke the vale?
Or who so hardy to declare
Disease and death ne'er enter there?
   Do pains or sickness here invade?
Man tenders me his chearful aid.
For who beholds his hungry beast,
But grants him some supply at least?
Int'rest shall prompt him to pursue
What inclination would not do.

Say, had I been the desert's foal,
Thro' life estrang'd to man's control;
What service had I done on earth,
Or who could profit by my birth?
My back had ne'er sustain'd thy weight,
My chest ne'er known thy waggon's freight;
But now my several powers combine
To answer Nature's ends and thine.
I'm useful thus in every view—
Oh! could I say the same of you!

   Superior evils had ensu'd,
With prescience had I been endu'd.
Ills, tho' at distance seen, destroy,
Or sicken every present joy.
We relish every new delight,
When future griefs elude our sight.
To blindness then what thanks are due!
It makes each single comfort two.
The colt, unknown to pain and toil,
Anticipates tomorrow's smile.
Yon lamb enjoys the present hour,
As stranger to the butcher's power.

                      Your's

FABLE VI.

Your's is a wild Utopian scheme,
A boy would blush to own your dream.
Be your profession what it will,
No province is exempt from ill.
Quite from the cottage to the throne,
Stations have sorrows of their own.
Why should a peasant then explore
What longer heads ne'er found before?
Go, preach my doctrine to your son,
By your's, the lad would be undone.
But whether he regards or not,
Your lecture would be soon forgot.
The hopes which gull'd the parent's breast,
Ere long will make his son their jest.
Tho' now these cobweb cheats you spurn,
Yet every man's a dupe in turn.
And wisely so ordain'd, indeed,
(Whate'er philosophers may plead),
Else life would stagnate at its source,
And Man, and Horse decline the course.

 Then bid young Ralpho never mind it,
But take the world as he shall find it.

TALES.

The LAMB and the PIG.

CONSULT the Moralist, you'll find
That education forms the mind.
But education ne'er supply'd
What ruling nature hath deny'd.
If you'll the following page pursue,
My tale shall prove this doctrine true.

Since to the muse all brutes belong,
The Lamb shall usher in my song;
Whose snowy fleece adorn'd her skin,
Emblem of native white within.
Meekness and love possess'd her soul,
And innocence had crown'd the whole.

It chanc'd, in some unguarded hour,
(Ah! purity, precarious flower!
Let maidens of the present age
Tremble, when they peruse my page.)

It chanc'd upon a luckless day,
The little wanton, full of play,
Rejoic'd a thymy bank to gain,
But short the triumphs of her reign!
The treacherous slopes her fate foretell,
And soon the pretty trifler fell.
Beneath, a dirty ditch impress'd
Its mire upon her spotless vest.
What greater ill cou'd lamb betide,
The butcher's barbarous knife beside?

 The shepherd, wounded with her cries,
Strait to the bleating sufferer flies.
The lambkin in his arms he took,
And bore her to a neighbouring brook.
The silver streams her wool refin'd,
Her fleece in virgin whiteness shin'd.

 Cleans'd from pollution's every stain,
She join'd her fellows on the plain;
And saw afar the stinking shore,
But ne'er approach'd those dangers more.
The shepherd bless'd the kind event,
And view'd his flock with sweet content.

To market next he shap'd his way,
And bought provisions for the day.
But made, for winter's rich supply,
A purchase from a farmer's sty.
The children round their parent crowd,
And testify their mirth aloud.
They saw the stranger with surprise,
And all admir'd his little eyes.
Familiar grown he shar'd their joys,
Shar'd too the porridge with the boys.
The females o'er his dress preside,
They wash his face and scour his hide.
But daily more a Swine he grew,
For all these housewives e'er could do.
    Hence let my youthful reader know,
That once a hog, and always so.

DEATH *and the* RAKE.

A Dutch Tale.

WHEN pleasures court the human heart,
    Oh! 'tis reluctant work to part.
Are we with griefs and pains oppress'd?
Woe says that Death's a welcome guest?
Tho' sure to cure our evils all,
He's the last doctor we wou'd call.
We think, if he arrives at morn,
'Tis hard to die, as soon as born.
Or if the conqueror invade,
When life projects the evening shade,
Do we not meditate delay,
And still request a longer stay?
We shift our homes, we change the air,
And double, like the hunted hare.
Thus be it morn, or night, or noon,
Come when he will, he comes too soon!

You wish my subject I wou'd wave,
The preface is so very grave.
Come then, my friend, I'll change my style,
And couch instruction with a smile.
But promise, ere I tell my tale,
The serious moral shall prevail.

Vanbruin dy'd—his son, we're told,
Succeeded to his father's gold.
Flush'd with his wealth, the thoughtless blade
Despis'd frugality, and trade;
Left Amsterdam with eager haste,
Dress, and the Hague, engross'd his taste.

Ere long his passion chang'd its shape,
He grew enamour'd with the grape.
Frequented much a house of cheer,
Just like our fools of fortune here;
With sots and harlots fond to join,
And revel o'er his midnight wine.

Once on a time the bowls had flow'd,
Quite till the morning cock had crow'd.
When Death, at every hour awake,
Enter'd the room, and claim'd the rake.

The

The youth's complexion spoke his fears,
Soft stole adown his cheek the tears.
At length the anguish of his breast
With fault'ring tongue he thus express'd.

 Thou king of terrors, hear my prayer,
And condescend for once to spare.
Let me thy clemency engage,
New to the world, and green in age.
When life no pleasures can dispense,
Or pleasures pall upon the sense;
When the eye feels departing sight,
And rolls its orb in vain for light;
When music's joys no longer cheer
The sick'ning heart, or heavy ear;
Or when my aching limbs forbear,
In sprightly balls to join the fair;
I'll not repeat my suit to Death,
But chearfully resign my breath.

 Done, says the monarch—be it so;
Observe—you promise then to go!

 What favour such protracted date
From the stern minister of fate!

Your wonder will be greater foon,
To hear the wretch perverts the boon.
Who, during years beyond a fcore,
Ne'er thought upon his promife more!

But were thefe terms by Death forgot?
Ah! no—again he feeks the fot.
The wretch was in the tavern found,
With a few gouty friends around.
Dropfy had feiz'd his legs and thighs,
Palfy his hands, and rheum his eyes.
When thus the king—Intemperate elf,
Thus, by debauch, to dupe yourfelf.
What! are my terrors fpurn'd by thee!
Thou fool! to trifle thus with me!
You afk'd before for length of days,
Only to riot various ways.
What were thy pleas but then a fneer?
I'll now retort with jeft fevere.

Read this fmall print, the monarch cries—
You mock me, fir, the man replies.
I fcarce could read when in my prime,
And now my fight's impair'd by time.

Sure you confider not my age—
I can't difcern a fingle page.
And when my friends the bottle pafs,
I fcarce can fee to fill my glafs.

Here, take this nut, obferve it well—
'Tis my command you crack the fhell.

How can fuch orders be obey'd?
My grinders, fir, are quite decay'd.
My teeth can fcarce divide my bread,
And not a found one in my head!

But Death, who more farcaftic grew,
Difclos'd a violin to view;
Then loud he call'd, Old Boy, advance,
Stretch out your legs, and lead the dance.

The man rejoin'd—When age furrounds,
How can the ear diftinguifh founds?
Are not my limbs unwieldy grown?
Are not my feet as cold as ftone?
Dear fir, take pity on my ftate—
My legs can fcarce fupport my weight!

Death drops the quaint, infulting joke,
And meditates the fatal ftroke.

Affuming

Assuming all his terrors now,
He speaks with anger on his brow.
　Is thus my lenity abus'd,
And dare you hope to stand excus'd ?
You've spent your time, that pearl of price !
To the detested ends of vice.
Purchas'd your short-liv'd pleasures dear,
And seal'd your own destruction here.
Inflam'd your reckoning too above,
By midnight bowls, and lawless love.
Warning, you know, I gave betimes—
Now go, and answer for your crimes.
　Oh ! my good lord, repress the blow—
I am not yet prepar'd to go.
And let it, sir, be further told,
That not a neighbour thinks me old.
My hairs are now but turning grey,
I am not sixty, sir, till May.
Grant me the common date of men,
I ask but threescore years and ten.
　Dar'st thou, prevaricating knave,
Insult the monarch of the grave ?

　　　　　　　　　　I claim

I claim thy solemn contract past—
Wherefore this moment is thy last.
  Thus having said, he speeds his dart,
And cleaves the hoary dotard's heart.

The second ODE *of the second Book of* HORACE.
      Inscribed to T. V. *Esq.*

DEAR youth, to hoarded wealth a foe,
    Riches with faded lustre glow;
Yes, dim the treasures of the mine,
Unless with temperate use they shine.
This stamps a value on the gold,
So Proculeius thought of old.

  Soon as this generous Roman saw
His father's sons proscrib'd by law,
The knight discharg'd a parent's part,
They shar'd his fortune and his heart.
Hence stands consign'd a brother's name
To immortality and fame.
                            Wou'd

Wou'd you true empire afcertain?
Curb all immoderate luft of gain.
This is the beft ambition known,
A greater conqueft than a throne.
For know, fhould Avarice controul,
Farewell the triumphs of the foul.

This is a dropfy of the mind,
Refembling the corporeal kind;
For who with this difeafe are curft,
The more they drink, the more they thirft.
Indulgence feeds their bloated veins,
And pale-ey'd, fighing languor reigns.

Virtue, who differs from the crowd,
Rejects the covetous and proud;
Difdains the wild ambitious breaft,
And fcorns to call a monarch bleft;
Labours to refcue truth and fenfe
From fpecious founds, and vain pretence.

Virtue

Virtue to that diſtinguiſh'd few,
Gives royalty, and conqueſt too;
That wiſe minority, who own,
And pay their tribute to her throne;
Who view with undeſiring eyes,
And ſpurn that wealth which miſers prize.

The Tenth ODE *of the ſecond* BOOK.

WOU'D you, my friend, true bliſs obtain?
    Nor preſs the coaſt, nor tempt the main.
In open ſeas loud tempeſts roar,
And treacherous rocks begirt the ſhore.

Hatred to all extremes is ſeen,
In thoſe who love the golden mean,
They nor in palaces rejoice,
Nor is the ſordid cot their choice.

The middle state of life is best,
Exalted stations find no rest;
Storms shake th' aspiring pine, and tower,
And mountains feel the thunder's power.

The mind prepar'd for each event,
In every state maintains content.
She hopes the best, when storms prevail,
Nor trusts too far the prosperous gale.

Shou'd time returning winters bring,
Returning winter yields to spring.
Shou'd darkness shroud the present skies,
Hereafter brighter suns shall rise.

When Pæan shoots his fiery darts,
Disease and death transfix our hearts;
But oft the God withholds his bow,
In pity to the race below.

When clouds the angry heavens deform,
Be ſtrong, and brave the ſwelling ſtorm;
Amidſt proſperity's full gales
Be humble, and contract your ſails.

EPITAPHS.

READER, approach my urn—thou need'st not fear
Th' extorted promise of one plaintive tear,
To mourn thy unknown friend—From me thou'lt learn
More than a Plato taught—the grand concern
Of mortals!—Wrapt in pensive thought, survey
This little freehold of unthinking clay,
And know thy end!
Tho' young, tho' gay, this scene of death explore,
Alas! the young, the gay is now no more!

On ROBERT CLAVERING, M. B.

OH! come, who know the childless parent's sigh,
The bleeding bosom, and the streaming eye;
Who feel the wounds a dying friend imparts,
When the last pang divides two social hearts.

This weeping marble claims the generous tear,
Here lies the friend, the son, and all that's dear.
 He fell full-blossom'd in the pride of youth,
The nobler pride of science, worth, and truth.
Calm and serene he view'd his mouldering clay,
Nor fear'd to go, nor fondly wish'd to stay.
And when the king of terrors he descry'd,
Kiss'd the stern mandate, bow'd his head, and dy'd.

On COLONEL GARDINER,

Who was slain in the Battle at Preston Pans, 1745.

WHILE fainter merit asks the powers of verse,
 Our faithful line shall GARDINER's worth rehearse.
The bleeding hero, and the martyr'd saint,
Transcends the poet's pen, the herald's paint.
His the best path to fame that e'er was trod,
And surely his a glorious road to God.

On Mr. SIBLEY,

Of Studham.

HERE lies an honest man! without pretence
    To more than prudence, and to common sense;
Who knew no vanity, disguise, nor art,
Who scorn'd all language foreign to the heart.
Diffusive as the light his bounty spread,
Cloath'd were the naked, and the hungry fed.
  "These be his honours!" honours that disclaim
The blazon'd scutcheon, and the herald's fame!
Honours! which boast defiance to the grave,
Where, spite of Anstis, rots the garter'd knave.

On a LADY, who had laboured under a Cancer.

STRANGER, these dear remains contain'd a mind
As infants guileless, and as angels kind.
                            Ripening

EPITAPHS. 55

Ripening for heav'n, by pains and sufferings try'd,
To pain superior, and unknown to pride.
Calm and serene beneath affliction's rod,
Because she gave her willing heart to God.
Because she trusted in her Saviour's pow'r,
Hence firm and fearless in the dying hour!
   No venal muse this faithful picture draws,
Blest saint! desert like yours extorts applause.
Oh! let a weeping friend discharge his due,
His debt to worth, to excellence, and you!

VARIOUS PIECES.

An Invocation of Happiness, after the Oriental Manner of Speech.

1. TELL me, O thou fairest among virgins, where dost thou lay thy meek contented head?

2. Dost thou dwell upon the mountains; dost thou make thy couch in the vallies?

3. In the still watches of the night have I thought upon my fair-one; yea, in the visions of the night have I pursued thee.

4. When I awoke, my meditation was upon thee, and the day was spent in search after thy embraces.

5. Why dost thou flee from me, as the tender hind, or the young roe upon the hills?

VARIOUS PIECES. 57

6. Without thy prefence in vain blufhes the rofe, in vain glows the ruby, the cinnamon breatheth its fragrance in vain.

7. Shall I make thee a houfe of the rich cedars of Lebanon? fhall I perfume it with all the fpices of Arabia? Wilt thou be tempted with Sabean odours, with myrrh, frankincenfe, and aloes?

8. Doth my fair-one delight in palaces—doth fhe gladden the hearts of kings? The palaces are not a meet refidence for my beloved—the princes of the earth are not favoured with the fmiles of her countenance.

9. My fair-one is meek and humble, fhe dwelleth among the cottages, fhe tendeth the fheep upon the mountains, and lieth down amidft the flocks. The lilies of the field are her couch, and the heavens her canopy.

10. Her words are fmoother than oil, more powerful than wine; her voice is as the voice of the turtle-dove.

11. Thou crowneft the innocence of the hufbandman, and the reward of virtue is with thee.

"*Time*

"*Time and Chance happeneth to them all.*"

Ecclefiaft. ch. ix. ver. 11.

READER, if fond of wonder and furprife,
Behold in me ten thoufand wonders rife.
Should I appear quite partial to my caufe,
Shout my own praife, and vindicate applaufe;
Do not arraign my modefty or fenfe,
Nor deem my character a vain pretence.
   Know then I boaft an origin and date
Coeval with the fun—without a mate
An offspring I beget in number more
Than all the crowded fands which form the fhore.
That inftant they are born, my precious breed
Ah me! expire—yet my departed feed
Enter like fpectres, with commiffion'd power,
The fecret chamber at the midnight hour;
Pervade alike the palace, and the fhed,
The ftatefman's clofet, and the ruftic's bed;
Serene and fweet, like envoys from the fkies,
To all the good, the virtuous, and the wife;

But to the vicious breast remorse they bring,
And bite like serpents, or like scorpions sting.
  Being and birth to sciences I give,
By me they rise thro' infancy and live;
By me meridian excellence display,
And, like autumnal fruits, by me decay.
When poets, and when painters are no more,
And all the feuds of rival wits are o'er;
'Tis mine to fix their merit and their claim,
I judge their works to darkness or to fame.
  I am a monarch, whose victorious hands
No craft eludes, no regal power withstands.
My annals prove such mighty conquests won,
As shame the puny feats of Philip's son.
But tho' a king, I seldom sway alone,
The goddess Fortune often shares my throne.
The human eye detects our blended rule,
Here we exalt a knave, and there a fool.
Ask you what powers our sovereign laws obey?
Creation is our empire—we convey
Sceptres and crowns at will—as we ordain,
Kings abdicate their thrones, and peasants reign.

Lovers to us addrefs the fervent prayer;
'Tis ours to foften or fubdue the fair:
We now like angels fmile, and now deftroy,
Now bring, or blaft, the long-expected joy.
At our fair fhrine ambitious churchmen bow,
And crave the mitre to adorn the brow.
Go to the inns of court—the learned drudge
Implores our friendfhip to commence a judge.
Go, and confult the fons of Warwick Lane;
They own our favours, and adore our reign.
Theirs is the gold, 'tis true—but all men fee
Our claim is better founded to the fee.

Reader, thus fublunary worlds we guide,
Thus o'er your natal planets we prefide.
Kingdoms and kings are ours—to us they fall,
We carve their fortunes, and difpofe of all.
Nor think that kings alone engrofs our choice,
The cobler fits attentive to our voice.

But fince my colleague is a fickle fhe,
Abjure my colleague, and depend on me.
Either fhe fees not, or with partial eyes,
Either fhe grants amifs, or fhe denies.

But

But I, who pity thofe that wear her chain,
Scorn the capricious meafures of her reign;
In every gift, and every grace excel,
And feldom fail their hopes, who ufe me well.
Yet tho' in me unnumber'd treafures fhine,
Superior to the rich Peruvian mine!
Tho' men to my indulgence hourly owe
The choiceft of their comforts here below:
(For men's beft tenure, as the world agree,
Is all a perquifite deriv'd from me)
Still man's my foe! ungrateful man, I fay,
Who meditates my murder every day.
What various fcenes of death do men prepare!
And what affaffinations plot the fair!
But know affuredly, who treat me ill,
Who mean to rob me, or who mean to kill;
Who view me with a cold regardlefs eye,
And let my favours pafs unheeded by;
They fhall lament their folly when too late;
So mourns the prodigal his loft eftate!

    While they who with fuperior forethought bleft,
Store all my leffons in their faithful breaft;

(For

(For where's the prelate, who can preach like me,
With equal reasoning, and persuasive plea,)
Who know that I am always on my wings,
And never stay in compliment to kings;
Who therefore watch me with an eagle's sight,
Arrest my pinions, or attend my flight;
Or if perchance they loiter'd in the race,
Chide their slow footsteps, and improve their pace;
Yes, these are wisdom's sons, and when they die,
Their virtues shall exalt them to the sky.

An ENIGMA, *inscribed to Miss* P.

CLOE, I boast celestial date,
    Ere time began to roll;
So wide my power, my sceptre spurns
    The limits of the pole.

When from the mystic womb of night,
    The Almighty call'd the earth;
I smil'd upon the infant world,
    And grac'd the wondrous birth.

Thro' the vast realms of boundless space,
  I traverse uncontroll'd;
And starry orbs of proudest blaze
  Inscribe my name in gold.

There's not a monarch in the north
  But bends the suppliant knee;
The haughty sultan waves his power,
  And owns superior me.

Both by the savage and the faint
  My empire stands confest;
I thaw the ice on Greenland's coast,
  And fire the Scythian's breast.

To me the gay aërial tribes
  Their glittering plumage owe;
With all the variegated pride
  That decks the feather'd beau.

The meanest reptiles of the land
  My bounty too partake;
I paint the insect's trembling wing,
  And gild the crested snake.

Survey the nations of the deep,
  You'll there my power behold;
My pencil drew the pearly scale,
  And fin bedropt with gold.

I give the virgin's lip to glow,
  I claim the crimson dye;
Mine is the rose which spreads the cheek,
  And mine the brilliant eye.

Then speak, my fair; for surely thou
  My name canst best descry;
Who gave to thee with lavish hands
  What thousands I deny.

The FIRESIDE.

DEAR Cloe, while the bufy croud,
    The vain, the wealthy, and the proud,
  In folly's maze advance;
Tho' fingularity and pride
Be call'd our choice, we'll ftep afide,
  Nor join the giddy dance.

From the gay world we'll oft retire
To our own family and fire,
  Where love our hours employs;
No noify neighbour enters here,
No intermeddling ftranger near,
  To fpoil our heartfelt joys.

If folid happinefs we prize,
Within our breaft this jewel lies,
  And they are fools who roam;
The world hath nothing to beftow,
From our own felves our blifs muft flow,
  And that dear hut our home.

Of reſt was Noah's dove bereft,
When with impatient wing ſhe left
    That ſafe retreat, the ark;
Giving her vain excurſions o'er,
The diſappointed bird once more
    Explor'd the ſacred bark.

Tho' fools ſpurn Hymen's gentle powers,
We, who improve his golden hours,
    By ſweet experience know,
That marriage, rightly underſtood,
Gives to the tender and the good,
    A paradiſe below.

Our babes ſhall richeſt comforts bring;
If tutor'd right they'll prove a ſpring,
    Whence pleaſures ever riſe:
We'll form their minds with ſtudious care,
To all that's manly, good, and fair,
    And train them for the ſkies.

While

While they our wifeſt hours engage,
They'll joy our youth, ſupport our age,
   And crown our hoary hairs;
They'll grow in virtue every day,
And they our fondeſt loves repay,
   And recompenſe our cares.

No borrow'd joys! they're all our own,
While to the world we live unknown,
   Or by the world forgot:
Monarchs! we envy not your ſtate,
We look with pity on the Great,
   And bleſs our humble lot.

Our portion is not large, indeed,
But then how little do we need,
   For Nature's calls are few!
In this the art of living lies,
To want no more than may ſuffice,
   And make that little do.

We'll therefore relish with content,
Whate'er kind Providence has sent,
  Nor aim beyond our power;
For, if our stock be very small,
'Tis prudence to enjoy it all,
  Nor lose the present hour.

To be resign'd when ills betide,
Patient when favours are deny'd,
  And pleas'd with favours given;
Dear Cloe, this is wisdom's part,
This is that incense of the heart,
  Whose fragrance smells to heaven.

We'll ask no long-protracted treat,
Since winter-life is seldom sweet;
  But, when our feast is o'er,
Grateful from table we'll arise,
Nor grudge our sons, with envious eyes,
  The relics of our store.

VARIOUS PIECES.

Thus hand in hand thro' life we'll go;
Its checker'd paths of joy and woe
   With cautious steps we'll tread;
Quit its vain scenes without a tear,
Without a trouble, or a fear,
   And mingle with the dead.

While conscience, like a faithful friend,
Shall thro' the gloomy vale attend,
   And cheer our dying breath;
Shall, when all other comforts cease,
Like a kind angel whisper peace,
   And smooth the bed of death.

To some CHILDREN listening to a LARK.

SEE the Lark prunes his active wings,
   Rises to heaven, and soars, and sings.
His morning hymns, his mid-day lays,
Are one continued song of praise.

He speaks his Maker all he can,
And shames the silent tongue of man.
  When the declining orb of light
Reminds him of approaching night,
His warbling vespers swell his breast,
And as he sings he sinks to rest.
  Shall birds instructive lessons teach,
And we be deaf to what they preach?
  No, ye dear nestlings of my heart,
Go, act the wiser songster's part.
Spurn your warm couch at early dawn,
And with your God begin the morn.
To Him your grateful tribute pay
Thro' every period of the day.
To Him your evening songs direct;
His eye shall watch, his arm protect.
Tho' darkness reigns, He's with you still,
Then sleep, my babes, and fear no ill.

To a CHILD of five Years old.

FAIREST flower, all flowers excelling,
   Which in Milton's page we see;
Flowers of Eve's embower'd dwelling*
   Are, my fair one, types of thee.

Mark, my Polly, how the roses
   Emulate thy damask cheek;
How the bud its sweets discloses——
   Buds thy opening bloom bespeak.

Lilies are by plain direction
   Emblems of a double kind;
Emblems of thy fair complexion,
   Emblems of thy fairer mind.

But, dear girl, both flowers and beauty
   Blossom, fade, and die away;
Then pursue good sense and duty,
   Evergreens! which ne'er decay.

* Alluding to Milton's description of Eve's bower.

On Lord COBHAM's Garden.

IT puzzles much the fages' brains,
   Where Eden ftood of yore;
Some place it in Arabia's plains,
   Some fay it is no more.

But Cobham can thefe tales confute,
   As all the curious know;
For he hath prov'd, beyond difpute,
   That Paradife is Stow.

TOMORROW.

Pereunt et imputantur.

TOMORROW, didft thou fay!
   Methought I heard Horatio fay, Tomorrow.
Go to—I will not hear of it—Tomorrow!
'Tis a fharper, who ftakes his penury
Againft thy plenty—who takes thy ready cafh,
And pays thee nought but wifhes, hopes, and promifes,

The currency of idiots. Injurious bankrupt,
That gulls the easy creditor!—Tomorrow!
It is a period nowhere to be found
In all the hoary regifters of time,
Unless perchance in the fool's calendar.
Wisdom disclaims the word, nor holds society
With those who own it. No, my Horatio,
'Tis Fancy's child, and Folly is its father;
Wrought of such stuff as dreams are; and baseless
As the fantastic visions of the evening.

But soft, my friend——arrest the present moments;
For be assur'd, they all are arrant tell-tales;
And tho' their flight be silent, and their path trackless
As the wing'd couriers of the air,
They post to heaven, and there record thy folly.
Because, tho' station'd on the important watch,
Thou, like a sleeping, faithless sentinel,
Didst let them pass unnotic'd, unimprov'd.
And know, for that thou slumber'dst on the guard,
Thou shalt be made to answer at the bar
For every fugitive: and when thou thus
Shalt stand impleaded at the high tribunal

Of hood-winkt justice, who shall tell thy audit?
   Then stay the present instant, dear Horatio;
Imprint the marks of wisdom on its wings.
'Tis of more worth than kingdoms! far more precious
Than all the crimson treasures of life's fountain!———
Oh! let it not elude thy grasp, but, like
The good old patriarch upon record,
Hold the fleet angel fast until he bless thee.

An Allusion to HORACE, *Ode* XVI. *Book* II.
    Inscribed to H. W. *Esq.*

    Otium divos rogat in patenti
    Prensus Ægæo, simul atra nubes
    Condidit lunam, neque certa fulgent
             Sidera nautis, &c.

SAY, heavenly Quiet, propitious nymph of light,
   Why art thou thus conceal'd from human sight?
Tir'd of life's follies, fain I'd gain thy arms,
Oh! take me panting to thy peaceful charms;
Sooth my wild soul, in thy soft fetters caught,
And calm the surges of tumultuous thought.

                   Thee,

VARIOUS PIECES.

 Thee, goddess, thee all states of life implore,
The merchant seeks thee on the foreign shore:
Thro' frozen zones and burning isles he flies,
And tempts the various horrors of the skies.
Nor frozen zones, nor burning isles control
That thirst of gain, that fever of the soul.
But mark the change—impending storms affright,
Array'd in all the majesty of night—
The raging winds, discharg'd their mystic caves,
Roar the dire signal to th' insulting waves.
The foaming legions charge the ribs of oak,
And the pale fiend presents at every stroke.
To Thee the unhappy wretch in pale despair
Bends the weak knee, and lifts the hand in prayer;
Views the sad cheat, and swears he'll ne'er again
Range the hot clime, or trust the faithless main,
Or own so mean a thought, that Thou art brib'd
  by gain.
 To Thee the harness'd chief devotes his breath,
And braves the thousand avenues of death;
Now red with fury seeks th' embattled plain,
Wades floods of gore, and scales the hills of slain;
           Now

Now on the fort with winged vengeance falls,
And tempts the sevenfold thunders of the walls.
Mistaken man! the nymph of peace disdains
The roar of cannons, and the smoke of plains:
With milder incense let thy altars blaze,
And in a softer note attempt her praise.
What various herds attend the virgin's gate,
Abject in wealth, and impotent in state!
A crowd of offerings on the altar lie,
And idly strive to tempt her from the sky:
But here the rich magnificence of kings
Are specious trifles all, and all unheeded things.
No outward show celestial bosoms warms,
The gaudy purple boasts inglorious charms;
The gold here, conscious of its abject birth,
Only presumes to be superior earth.
In vain the gem its sparkling tribute pays,
And meanly tremulates in borrow'd rays.
On these the nymph with scornful smiles looks down,
Nor e'er elects the favourite of a crown.
Supremely great, she views us from afar,
Nor deigns to own a sultan or a czar.

Did

Did real happiness attend on state,
How would I pant and labour to be great!
To court I'd hasten with impetuous speed;
But to be great's to be a wretch indeed.

  I speak of sacred truths; believe me, Hugh,
The real wants of nature are but few.
Poor are the charms of gold—a generous heart
Would blush to own a bliss, that these impart.
'Tis he alone the muse dares happy call,
Who with superior thought enjoys his little all.
Within his breast no frantic passions roll,
Soft are the motions of the virtuous soul.
The night in silken slumbers glides away,
And a sweet calm leads in the smiling day.

  What antic notions form the human mind!
Perversely mad, and obstinately blind.
Life in its large extent is scarce a span,
Yet, wondrous frenzy! great designs we plan,
And shoot our thoughts beyond the date of man.

  Man, that vain creature's but a wretched elf,
And lives at constant enmity with self;

Swears

Swears to a southern climate he'll repair,
But who can change the mind by changing air?
Italia's plains may purify the blood,
And with a nobler purple paint the flood;
But can soft zephyrs aid th' ill-shapen thigh,
Or form to beauty the distorted eye?
Can they with life inform the thoughtless clay?
Then a kind gale might waft my cares away.
Where roves the muse?—'tis all a dream, my friend,
All a wild thought—for care, that ghastly fiend,
That mighty prince of the infernal powers,
Haunts the still watches of the midnight hours.
In vain the man the night's protection sought,
Care stings like pois'nous asps to fury wrought,
And wakes the mind to all the pains of thought.
Not the wing'd ship, that sweeps the level main,
Not the young roe that bounds along the plain,
Are swift as Care—that monster leaves behind
The aerial courser and the fleeter wind;
Thro' every clime performs a constant part,
And sheaths its painful daggers in the heart.

                                      Ah!

Ah! why should man an idle game pursue,
To future May-be's stretch the distant view?
May more exalted thoughts our hours employ,
And wisely strive to taste the present joy.
Life's an inconstant sea—the prudent ply
With every oar to improve th' auspicious sky:
But if black clouds the angry heav'ns deform,
A chearful mind will sweeten every storm.
Tho' fools expect their joys to flow sincere,
Yet none can boast eternal sunshine here.

 The youthful chief, that like a summer flower
Shines a whole life in one precarious hour,
Impatient of restraint demands the fight,
While painted triumphs swim before his sight.
Forbear, brave youth, thy bold designs give o'er,
Ere the next morn shall dawn, thou'lt be no more;
Invidious death shall blast thy opening bloom,
Scarce blown, thou fad'st, scarce born, thou meet'st a tomb.

 What tho', my friend, the young are swept away,
Untimely cropt in the proud blaze of day;

Yet when life's spring on purple wings is flown,
And the brisk flood a noisome puddle grown;
When the dark eye shall roll its orb for light,
And the roll'd orb confess impervious night;
When once untun'd the ear's contorted cell,
The silver cords unbrace the sounding shell;
Thy sick'ning soul no more a joy shall find,
Music no more shall stay thy lab'ring mind.
The breathing canvas glows in vain for thee,
In vain it blooms a gay eternity.
With thee the statue's boasts of life are o'er,
And Cæsar animates the brass no more.
The flaming ruby, and the rich brocade,
The sprightly ball, the mimic masquerade
Now charm in vain—in vain the jovial god
With blushing goblets plies the dormant clod.

 Then why thus fond to draw superfluous breath,
When every gasp protracts a painful death?
Age is a ghastly scene, cares, doubts, and fears,
One dull rough road of sighs, groans, pains, and tears.

Let not ambitious views ufurp thy foul,
Ambition, friend, ambition grafps the pole.
The luftful eye on wealth's bright ftrand you fix,
And figh for grandeur and a coach and fix;
With golden ftars you long to blend your fate,
And with the garter'd lordling flide in ftate.
An humbler theme my penfive hours employs,
(Hear ye fweet heavens, and fpeed the diftant joys!
Of thefe poffefs'd I'd fcorn to court renown,
Or blefs the happy coxcombs of the town.)
To me, ye gods, thefe only gifts impart,
An eafy fortune, and a cheerful heart;
A little mufe, and innocently gay,
In fportive fong to trifle cares away.
Two wifhes gain'd, love forms the laft and beft,
And heaven's bright mafter-piece fhall crown the rest.

An EPITAPH *upon Mr.* THOMAS STRONG, *who died on the* 26*th of December,* 1736.

IN action prudent, and in word sincere,
In friendship faithful, and in honour clear;
Thro' life's vain scenes the same in every part,
A steady judgment, and an honest heart.
Thou vaunt'st no honours—all thy boast a mind
As infants guileless, and as angels kind.
    When ask'd to whom these lovely truths belong,
Thy friends shall answer, weeping, " Here lies
    " STRONG."

EPITAPH *upon Miss* GEE,

Who died October 25, 1736, *Ætat.* 28.

BEAUTEOUS, nor known to pride, to friends sincere,
Mild to thy neighbour, to thyself severe;
                                        Unstain'd

Unstain'd thy honour—and thy wit was such,
Knew no extremes, nor little, nor too much.
Few were thy years, and painful thro' the whole,
Yet calm thy passage, and serene thy soul.

Reader, amidst these sacred crowds that sleep*,
View this once lovely form, nor grudge to weep.—
O death, all terrible! how sure thy hour!
How wide thy conquests! and how fell thy power!
When youth, wit, virtue, plead for longer reign,
When youth, when wit, when virtue plead in vain;
Stranger, then weep afresh—for know this clay
Was once the good, the wise, the beautiful, the gay.

REBUS.

THAT awful name which oft inspires
    Impatient hopes, and fond desires,
Can to another pain impart,
And thrill with fear the shudd'ring heart.

* The author is supposed to be inscribing the character of the deceased upon her tomb, and therefore " crowds that " sleep," mean the dead.

This myſtic word is often read
O'er the ſtill chambers of the dead.
Say, what contains the breathleſs clay,
When the fleet ſoul is wing'd away?—
Thoſe marble monuments proclaim
My little wily wanton's name.

TOMBS.

R E B U S.

THE golden ſtem, with generous aid,
    Supports and feeds the fruitful blade.
The queen, who rul'd a thankleſs iſle,
And gladden'd thouſands with her ſmile
(When the well-manag'd pound of gold
Did more, than now the ſum thrice told;)
This ſtem of Ceres, and the fair
Of Stuart's houſe, a name declare,
Where goodneſs is with beauty join'd,
Where queen and goddeſs both combin'd
To form an emblem of the mind.

REBUS.

REBUS.

THE light-footed female that bounds o'er the hills,
That feeds among lilies, and drinks of the rills,
  And is fam'd for being tender and true;
Which Solomon deemed a simile rare,
To liken the two pretty breasts of his fair,
  Is the name of the nymph I pursue.

R O E.

ANOTHER.

TELL me the fair, if such a fair there be,
  Said Venus to her son, that rivals me.
Mark the tall tree, cried Cupid to the Dame,
That from its silver bark derives its name;
The studious insect, that, with wondrous pow'rs,
Extracts mysterious sweets from fragrant flow'rs;
Proclaim the nymph to whom all hearts submit,
Whose sweetness softens majesty and wit.

A S H B Y.

VARIOUS PIECES

Some hasty Rhimes on SLEEP.

MYSTERIOUS deity, impart
From whence thou com'st, and what thou art.
I feel thy pow'r, thy reign I bless,
But what I feel, I can't express.
Thou bind'st my limbs, but canstn't restrain
The busy workings of the brain.
   All nations of the air and land
Ask the soft blessing at thy hand.
The reptiles of the frozen zone
Are close attendants on thy throne;
Where painted basilisks infold
Their azure scales in rolls of gold.
   The slave, that's destin'd to the oar,
In one kind vision swims to shore;
The lover meets the willing fair,
And fondly grasps impassive air.
Last night the happy miser told
Twice twenty thousand pounds in gold.

The purple tenant of the crown
Implores thy aid on beds of down:
While Lubbin, and his healthy bride,
Obtain what monarchs are denied.

The garter'd statesman thou wouldst own,
But rebel conscience spurns thy throne;
Braves all the poppies of the fields,
And the fam'd gum * that Turkey yields.

While the good man, oppress'd with pain,
Shall court thy smiles, nor sue in vain.
Propitious thou'lt his prayer attend,
And prove his guardian and his friend.
Thy faithful hands shall make his bed,
And thy soft arm support his head.

* Or rather inspissated juice, Opium.

A REBUS.

THE name of the monarch that abandon'd his throne,
Is the name of the fair, I prefer to his crown.

JAMES.

A SONG.

TELL me, my Cælia, why so coy,
   Of men so much afraid;
Cælia, 'tis better far to die
   A mother than a maid.

The rose, when past its damask hue,
   Is always out of favour;
And when the plum hath lost its blue,
   It loses too its flavour.

To vernal flow'rs the rolling years
   Returning beauty bring;
But faded once, thou'lt bloom no more,
   Nor know a second spring.

A SUNDAY

VARIOUS PIECES. 89

A Sunday Hymn, *in Imitation of Dr. Watts.*

THIS is the day the Lord of life
    Afcended to the fkies;
My thoughts, purfue the lofty theme,
    And to the heav'ns arife.

Let no vain cares divert my mind
    From this celeftial road;
Nor all the honours of the earth
    Detain my foul from God.

Think of the fplendors of that place,
    The joys that are on high;
Nor meanly reft contented here,
    With worlds beneath the fky.

Heav'n is the birth-place of the faints,
    To heav'n their fouls afcend;
Th' Almighty owns his favourite race,
    As father and as friend.

                                      Oh!

Oh! may these lovely titles prove
   My comfort and defence,
When the sick couch shall be my lot,
   And death shall call me hence.

An ODE on the MESSIAH.

1.

WHEN man had disobey'd his Lord,
   Vindictive Justice drew the sword;
" The rebel and his race shall die."
He spake, and thunders burst the sky.

2.

Lo! Jesus pard'ning grace displays,
Nor thunders roll, nor lightnings blaze,
Jesus, the Saviour stands confest,
In rays of mildest glories drest.

3.

As round Him prefs th' angelic crowd,
Mercy and Truth He calls aloud;
The fmiling cherubs wing'd to view,
Their pinions founded as they flew.

4.

" Ye favourites of the throne, arife,
" Bear the ftrange tidings thro' the fkies;
" Say, Man, th' apoftate rebel, lives;
" Say, Jefus bleeds, and Heav'n forgives."

5.

In pity to the fallen race,
I'll take their nature and their place;
I'll bleed, their pardon to procure,
I'll die, to make that pardon fure.

6.

Now Jefus leaves his bleft abode,
A Virgin's womb receives the God.
When the tenth moon had wan'd on earth,
A Virgin's womb difclos'd the birth.

7.

New praise employs th' ethereal throng,
Their golden harps repeat the song;
And angels waft th' immortal strains
To humble Bethl'em's happy plains.

8.

While there the guardians of the sheep
By night their faithful vigils keep,
Celestial notes their ears delight,
And floods of glory drown their sight.

9.

When Gabriel thus, " Exult, ye swains,
" Jesus, your own Messiah, reigns.
" Arise, the Royal Babe behold,
" Jesus, by ancient bards foretold.

10.

" To David's town direct your way,
" And shout, Salvation's born to-day;
" There, in a manger's mean disguise,
" You'll find the Sovereign of the skies."

VARIOUS PIECES.

11.

What joy Salvation's found imparts,
You beſt can tell, ye guilelefs hearts;
Whom no vain fcience led aftray,
Nor taught to fcorn Salvation's way.

12.

Tho' regal purple fpurns thefe truths,
Maintain your ground, ye chofen youths;
Brave the ſtern tyrant's lifted rod,
Nor bluſh to own a dying God.

13.

What! tho' the fages of the earth
Proudly difpute this wondrous birth;
Tho' learning mocks Salvation's voice,
Know, Heav'n applauds your wifer choice.

14.

Oh! be this wifer choice my own!
Bear me, fome feraph, to His throne,
Where the rapt foul diffolves away
In vifions of eternal day.

An ODE on the NEW YEAR.

1.

LORD of my life, inspire my song,
To Thee my noblest powers belong;
Grant me thy favourite seraph's flame,
To sing the glories of thy name.

2.

My birth, my fortune, friends, and health,
My knowledge too, superior wealth!
Lord of my life, to Thee I owe;
Teach me to practise what I know.

3.

Ten thousand favours claim my song,
And each demands an angel's tongue;
Mercy sits smiling on the wings
Of every moment as it springs.

4.

But oh! with infinite surprise
I see returning years arise;
When unimprov'd the former score,
Lord, wilt thou trust me still with more!

5.

Thousands this period hop'd to see;
Deny'd to thousands, granted me;
Thousands! that weep, and wish, and pray
For those rich hours I throw away.

6.

The tribute of my heart receive,
'Tis the poor *all* I have to give;
Should it prove faithless, Lord, I'd wrest
The bleeding traitor from my breast.

EPITAPH

EPITAPH

On JOHN *Duke of* BRIDGWATER,
Who died in the twenty-first Year of his Age, 1747-8.

INTENT to hear, and bounteous to bestow,
A mind that melted at another's woe;
Studious to act the self-approving part,
That midnight-music of the honest heart!
Those silent joys th' illustrious youth possess'd,
Those cloudless sunshines of the spotless breast!
From pride of peerage, and from folly free,
Life's early morn, fair Virtue! gave to thee;
Forbad the tear to steal from Sorrow's eye,
Bade anxious Poverty forget to sigh;
Like Titus, knew the value of a day,
And Want went smiling from his gates away.

 The rest were honours borrow'd from the throne;
These honours, EGERTON, were all thy own!

A FABLE.

A FABLE.

IT seems, an Owl, in days of yore,
Had turn'd a thousand volumes o'er.
His fame for literature extends,
And strikes the ears of partial friends.
They weigh'd the learning of the fowl,
And thought him a prodigious Owl!
From such applause what could betide?
It only cocker'd him in pride.
　Extoll'd for sciences and arts,
His bosom burn'd to shew his parts;
(No wonder that an Owl of spirit,
Mistook his vanity for merit.)
He shews insatiate thirst of praise,
Ambitious of the poet's bays.
Perch'd on Parnassus all night long,
He hoots a sonnet or a song;
And while the village hear his note,
They curse the screaming whore-son's throat.
　Amidst the darkness of the night,
Our feather'd poet wings his flight,

And, as capricious fate ordains,
A chimney's treach'rous summit gains;
Which much impair'd by wind and weather,
Down fall the bricks and bird together.

   The Owl expands his azure eyes,
And sees a Non-con's study rise;
The walls were deck'd with hallow'd bands
Of worthies, by th' engraver's hands;
All champions for the good old cause!
Whose conscience interfer'd with laws;
But yet no foes to king or people,
Tho' mortal foes to church and steeple.
Baxter, with apostolic grace,
Display'd his metzotinto face;
While here and there some luckier saint
Attain'd to dignity of paint.

   Rang'd in proportion to their size,
The books by due gradations rise.
Here the good Fathers lodg'd their trust;
There zealous Calvin slept in dust.
Here Pool his learned treasures keeps;
There Fox o'er dying martyrs weeps;

While reams on reams infatiate drink
Whole deluges of Henry's ink.
   Columns of sermons pil'd on high
Attract the bird's admiring eye.
Those works a good old age acquir'd,
Which had in manuscript expir'd;
For manuscripts, of fleeting date,
Seldom survive their infant state.
The healthiest live not half their days,
But die a thousand various ways;
Sometimes ingloriously apply'd
To purposes the Muse shall hide.
Or, should they meet no fate below,
How oft tobacco proves their foe!
Or else some cook purloins a leaf
To singe her fowl, or save her beef;
But sermons 'scape both fate and fire,
By congregational desire.
   Display'd at large upon the table
Was Bunyan's much-admir'd fable;
And as his Pilgrim sprawling lay,
It chanc'd the Owl advanc'd that way.

The bird explores the pious dream,
And plays a visionary scheme;
Determin'd, as he read the sage,
To copy from the tinker's page.

The thief now quits his learn'd abode,
And scales aloft the sooty road;
Flies to Parnassus' top once more,
Resolv'd to dream as well as snore;
And what he dreamt by day, the wight
In writing o'er, consumes the night.

Plum'd with conceit he calls aloud,
And thus bespeaks the purblind crowd;
Say not, that man alone's a poet,
Poets are Owls—my verse shall show it.
And while he read his labour'd lays,
His blue-ey'd brothers hooted praise.
But now his female mate by turns
With pity and with choler burns;
When thus her consort she address'd,
And all her various thoughts express'd.

Why, prithee, husband, rant no more,
'Tis time to give these follies o'er.

Be

Be wife, and follow my advice——
Go——catch your family some mice.
'Twere better to resume your trade,
And spend your nights in ambuscade.
What! if you fatten by your schemes,
And fare luxuriously in dreams!
While you ideal mice are carving,
I and my family are starving.
Reflect upon our nuptial hours,
Where will you find a brood like our's?
Our offspring might become a queen,
For finer Owlets ne'er were seen!

   'Ods—blue! the surly hob reply'd,
I'll amply for my heirs provide.
Why, Madge! when Colley Cibber dies,
Thou'lt see thy mate a Laur'ate rise;
For never poets held this place,
Except descendants of our race.

   But soft—the female sage rejoin'd—
Say you abjur'd the purring kind;
And nobly left inglorious rats
To vulgar owls, or sordid cats.

Say, you the healing art essay'd,
And piddled in the doctor's trade;
At least you'd earn us good provisions,
And better this than scribbling visions.
A due regard to me, or self,
Wou'd always make you dream of pelf;
And when you dreamt your nights away,
You'd realize your dreams by day.
Hence far superior gains wou'd rise,
And I be fat and you be wife.

 But, Madge, tho' I applaud your scheme,
You'd wish my patients still to dream!
Waking they'd laugh at my vocation,
Or disapprove my education;
And they detest your solemn hob,
Or take me for professor L——.

 Equipt with powder and with pill,
He takes his licence out to kill.
Practis'd in all a doctor's airs,
To Batson's senate he repairs,
Dress'd in his flowing wig of knowledge,
To greet his brethren of the college;

Takes

Takes up the papers of the day,
Perhaps for want of what to say;
Thro' ev'ry column he pursues,
Alike advertisements and news;
O'er lists of cures with rapture runs,
Wrought by Apollo's natural sons;
Admires the rich Hibernian stock
Of doctors, Henry, Ward, and Rock.
He dwells on each illustrious name,
And sighs at once for fees and fame.
Now, like the doctors of to-day,
Retains his puffers too in pay.
Around his reputation flew,
His practice with his credit grew,
At length the court receives the sage,
And lordlings in his cause engage.
He dupes, beside plebeian fowls,
The whole nobility of owls.
Thus ev'ry where he gains renown,
And fills his purse, and thins the town.

Addressed to a young LADY, *whose favourite Bird was almost killed by a fall from her Finger.*

AS Tiney, in a wanton mood,
   Upon his Lucy's finger stood,
     Ambitious to be free;
With breast elate he eager tries,
By flight to reach the distant skies,
     And gain his liberty.

Ah! luckless bird, what tho' caress'd,
And fondled in the fair one's breast,
     Taught e'en by her to sing;
Know that to check thy temper wild,
And make thy manners soft and mild,
     Thy mistress cut thy wing.

The feather'd tribe, who cleave the air,
Their weights by equal plumage bear,
     And quick escape our pow'r;
Not so with Tiney, dear delight,
His shorten'd wing repress'd his flight,
     And threw him on the floor.

                        Stunn'd

Stunn'd with the fall, he seem'd to die,
For quickly clos'd his sparkling eye,
    Scarce heav'd his pretty breast;
Alarmed for her favourite care,
Lucy assumes a pensive air,
    And is at heart distrest.

The stoic soul, in gravest strain,
May call these feelings light and vain,
    Which thus from fondness flow;
Yet, if the bard arightly deems,
'Tis nature's fount which feeds the streams
    That purest joys bestow.

So, shou'd it be fair Lucy's fate,
Whene'er she wills a change of state,
    To boast a mother's name;
These feelings then, thou charming maid,
In brightest lines shall be display'd,
    And praise uncensur'd claim.

RIDDLES.

RIDDLES.

FROM the dark caverns of the earth
Our family derive their birth;
By nature we appear to view
A rugged and a stubborn crew.
But Vulcan's brawny sons, by art,
Soften the hardness of our heart;
Give to a slender shape its grace,
And a bright polish to our face.
Thus education makes us mild,
Pliant and ductile as a child.

Survey the attire of man, you'll trace
Our friendship for the human race.
We love mankind, indeed we do,
Our actions prove our speeches true.
But what is wondrous strange to name,
The aged female is our flame.

When strength decays, and optics fail,
And cold and penury prevail,
Our labours spare the matron's sight,
We ask but faint supplies of light.
Kindly our ancient girls regale,
With food, with fuel, and with ale.
We, as associates to mankind,
All act our various parts assign'd.
No useless hands obstruct our schemes,
We suit our numbers to our themes;
Hence only two of us apply,
To form a bandage for the thigh;
But when the grey industrious Peg
Demands a vestment for the leg,
'Tis then in little crowds we join
To aid the matron's wise design.
Thus four or five of us you'll see,
And each as busy as a bee;
Besides a kind assistant near,
Which Peg had stuck athwart her ear.
  Now lasses, if our name you'll tell,
And vow you'll always use us well,

We'll

We'll grant your wish to change your life,
And make each fair a happy wife.

KNITTING NEEDLE.

ANOTHER.

1.

TO you, fair maidens, I address,
   Sent to adorn your life;
And she who first my name can guess,
   Shall first be made a wife.

2.

From the dark womb of mother earth,
   To mortals' aid I come;
But ere I can receive my birth,
   I many shapes assume.

3. Passive

3.

Paffive by nature, yet I'm made
  As active as the roe;
And oftentimes, with equal fpeed,
  Thro' flowery lawns I go.

4.

When wicked men their wealth confume,
  And leave their children poor,
To me their daughters often come,
  And I encreafe their ftore.

5.

The women of the wifer kind,
  Did never once refufe me;
But yet I never once could find
  That maids of honour ufe me.

6.

The lily hand and brilliant eye,
  May charm without my aid;
Beauty may ftrike the lover's eye,
  And love infpire the maid.

7.

But let the enchanting nymph be told,
  Unlefs I grace her life,
She muft have wondrous ftore of gold,
  Or make a wretched wife.

8.

Altho' I never hope to reft,
  With Chriftians I go forth;
And while they worfhip to the eaft,
  I proftrate to the north.

9.

If you fufpect hypocrify,
  Or think me infincere,
Produce the zealot, who, like me,
  Can tremble and adhere.

NEEDLE.

ANOTHER.

ANOTHER.

I AM by nature soft as silk,
By nature too as white as milk;
I am a constant friend to man,
And serve him every way I can.
When dipt in wax, or plung'd in oil,
I make his winter evenings smile:
By India taught I spread his bed,
Or deck his favourite Celia's head;
Her gayest garbs I oft compose,
And ah! sometimes, I wipe her nose.

COTTON.

ANOTHER.

I AM a small volume, and frequently bound
In silk, sattin, silver, or gold;
My worth and my praises the females resound,
By females my science is told.

My leaves are all scarlet, my letters are steel,
   Each letter contains a great treasure;
To the poor they spell lodging, fuel, and meal,
   To the rich, entertainment and pleasure.

The sempstress explores me by day and by night,
   Not a page but she turns o'er and o'er;
Tho' sometimes I injure the milliner's sight,
   Still I add to her credit and store.

'Tis true I am seldom regarded by men,
   Yet what would the males do without me?
Let them boast of their head, or boast of their pen,
   Still vain is their boast if they flout me.

NEEDLE BOOK.

PSALM

PSALM XIII.

OFFENDED Majesty! how long
   Wilt thou conceal thy face?
How long refuse my fainting soul
   The succours of thy grace?

While sorrow wrings my bleeding heart,
   And black despondence reigns,
Satan exults at my complaints,
   And triumphs o'er my pains.

Let thy returning spirit, Lord,
   Dispel the shades of night;
Smile on my poor deserted soul,
   My God, thy smiles are light.

While scoffers at thy sacred word
   Deride the pangs I feel,
Deem my religion insincere,
   Or call it useless zeal.

Yet will I ne'er repent my choice,
   I'll ne'er withdraw my truſt;
I know thee, Lord, a pow'rful friend,
   And kind, and wiſe, and juſt.

To doubt Thy goodneſs wou'd be baſe
   Ingratitude in me;
Paſt favours ſhall renew my hopes,
   And fix my faith in Thee.

Indulgent God! my willing tongue
   Thy praiſes ſhall prolong;
For oh! Thy bounty fires my breaſt,
   And rapture ſwells my ſong.

PSALM XLII.

WITH fierce deſire the hunted hart
   Explores the cooling ſtream;
Mine is a paſſion ſtronger far,
   And mine a nobler theme.

Yes, with superior fervors, Lord,
    I thirst to see thy face;
My languid soul would fain approach
    The fountains of thy grace.

Oh! the great plenty of thy house,
    The rich refreshments there!
To live an exile from thy courts
    O'erwhelms me with despair.

In worship when I join'd thy saints,
    How sweetly pass'd my days!
Prayer my divine employment then,
    And all my pleasure praise.

But now I'm lost to every joy,
    Because detain'd from Thee;
Those golden periods ne'er return,
    Or ne'er return to me.

Yet, O my soul, why thus deprest,
  And whence this anxious fear?
Let former favours fix thy trust,
  And check the rising tear.

When darkness and when sorrows rose,
  And press'd on every side,
Did not the Lord sustain thy steps,
  And was not God thy guide?

Affliction is a stormy deep,
  Where wave resounds to wave;
Tho' o'er my head the billows roll,
  I know the Lord can save.

Perhaps, before the morning dawns,
  He'll reinstate my peace;
For He, who bade the tempest roar,
  Can bid the tempest cease.

In the dark watches of the night
  I'll count his mercies o'er;
I'll praise him for ten thousand past,
  And humbly sue for more.

Then, O my soul, why thus deprest,
  And whence this anxious fear?
Let former favours fix thy trust,
  And check the rising tear.

Here will I rest, and build my hopes,
  Nor murmur at his rod;
He's more than all the world to me,
  My health, my life, my God!

The NIGHT PIECE.

HARK! the prophetic raven brings
  My summons on his boding wings;
The birds of night my fate foretel,
The prescient death-watch sounds my knell.

A solemn

A solemn darkness spreads the tomb,
But terrors haunt the midnight gloom;
Methinks a browner horror falls,
And silent spectres sweep the walls.

Tell me, my soul, oh tell me why
The faultering tongue, the broken sigh?
Thy manly cheeks bedew'd with tears,
Tell me, my soul, from whence these fears?

When conscious guilt arrests the mind,
Avenging furies stalk behind,
And sickly fancy intervenes,
To dress the visionary scenes.

Jesus, to thee I'll fly for aid,
Propitious Sun, dispel the shade;
All the pale family of fear
Would vanish were my Saviour here.

No more imagin'd spectres walk,
No more the doubtful echoes talk;
Soft zephyrs fan the neighbouring trees,
And meditation mounts the breeze.

How sweet these sacred hours of rest,
Fair portraits of the virtuous breast,
Where lawless lust, and passions rude,
And folly never dare intrude!

Be others' choice the sparkling bowl,
And mirth, the poison of the soul;
Or midnight dance, and public shows,
Parents of sickness, pains, and woes.

A nobler joy my thoughts design;
Instructive solitude, be mine;
Be mine that silent calm repast,
A chearful conscience to the last.

That tree which bears immortal fruit,
Without a canker at the root;
That friend which never fails the juſt,
When other friends deſert their truſt.

Come then, my ſoul, be this thy gueſt,
And leave to knaves and fools the reſt.
With this thou ever ſhalt be gay,
And night ſhall brighten into day.

With this companion in the ſhade,
Surely thou couldſt not be diſmay'd;
But if thy Saviour here were found,
All Paradiſe would bloom around.

" Had I a firm and laſting faith,
To credit what the Almighty ſaith,
I could defy the midnight gloom,
And the pale monarch of the tomb.

Though tempests drive me from the shore,
And floods descend, and billows roar;
Though death appears in every form,
My little bark should brave the storm.

Then if my God requir'd the life
Of brother, parent, child, or wife,
Lord, I should bless the stern decree,
And give my dearest friend to thee.

Amidst the various scenes of ills,
Each stroke some kind design fulfils;
And shall I murmur at my God,
When sovereign love directs the rod?

Peace, rebel-thoughts—I'll not complain,
My father's smiles suspend my pain;
Smiles—that a thousand joys impart,
And pour the balm that heals the smart.

Though Heaven afflicts, I'll not repine,
Each heart-felt comfort still is mine;
Comforts that shall o'er death prevail,
And journey with me through the vale.

Dear Jesus, smooth that rugged way,
And lead me to the realms of day,
To milder skies, and brighter plains,
Where everlasting sunshine reigns.

To the Rev. JAMES HERVEY, *on his Meditations.*

By a Physician.

TO form the taste, and raise the nobler part,
   To mend the morals, and to warm the heart;
To trace the genial source we Nature call,
And prove the God of Nature friend of all;
Hervey for this his mental landscape drew,
And sketch'd the whole creation out to view.

Th' enamell'd bloom, and variegated flow'r,
Whose crimson changes with the changing hour;
The humble shrub, whose fragrance scents the morn,
With buds disclosing to the early dawn;
The oaks that grace Britannia's mountains' side,
And spicy Lebanon's superior * pride;
All loudly sov'reign excellence proclaim,
And animated worlds confess the same.

The azure fields that form th' extended sky,
The planetary globes that roll on high,
And solar orbs, of proudest blaze, combine
To act subservient to the great design.
Men, angels, seraphs, join the gen'ral voice,
And in the Lord of Nature all rejoice.

His the grey winter's venerable guise,
Its shrouded glories, and instructive skies †;
His the snow's plumes, that brood the sick'ning blade;
His the bright pendant that impearls the glade;
The waving forest, or the whisp'ring brake;
The surging billow, or the sleeping lake.

* The Cedar.   † Referring to the Winter-Piece.

The fame who pours the beauties of the spring,
Or mounts the whirlwind's desolating wing.
The fame who smiles in Nature's peaceful form,
Frowns in the tempest, and directs the storm.

  'Tis thine, bright teacher, to improve the age;
'Tis thine, whose life's a comment on thy page;
Thy happy page! whose periods sweetly flow,
Whose figures charm us, and whose colours glow:
Where artless piety pervades the whole,
Refines the genius, and exalts the soul.
For let the witling argue all he can,
It is religion still that makes the man.
'Tis this, my friend, that streaks our morning bright;
'Tis this that gilds the horrors of the night.
When wealth forsakes us, and when friends are few;
When friends are faithless, or when foes pursue;
'Tis this that wards the blow, or stills the smart,
Disarms affliction, or repels its dart;
Within the breast bids purest rapture rise;
Bids smiling conscience spread her cloudless skies.

  When the storm thickens, and the thunder rolls,
When the earth trembles to th' affrighted poles,

The virtuous mind nor doubts nor fears affail;
For ftorms are zephyrs, or a gentler gale.
  And when difeafe obftructs the lab'ring breath;
When the heart fickens, and each pulfe is death;
E'en then religion fhall fuftain the juft,
Grace their laft moments, nor defert their duft.
    Auguft 5, 1748.

LINES *under a* SUN-DIAL *in the Church-yard at* THORNBY.

MARK well my fhade, and ferioufly attend
    The filent leffon of a common friend—
Since time and life fpeed haftily away,
And neither can recal the former day,
Improve each fleeting hour before 'tis paft,
And know, each fleeting hour may be thy laft.

To the Memory
Of the Reverend Mr. SAMUEL CLARK,
Who died December the 26*th, aged* 42.

IN all the intercourses of humanity
He was upright, prudent, and courteous,
Compassionate, kind, and beneficent.
In opinion
Candid, diffident, and judicious.
In argument
Calm, strong, and persuasive.
Under difficulties and sorrows
Collected, firm, and resign'd.
In friendship
Faithful, entertaining, and instructive.
In his ministerial capacity
He possessed every valuable and happy talent
To rectify the judgment, and improve the heart.

He was learned without pride,
And pious without oftentation;
Zealous and indefatigable to advance the intereſt
Of true religion,
And the everlaſting welfare of thoſe who were entruſted
To his paſtoral care.

What! tho' ſuch various worth is ſeldom known,
No adulation rears this ſacred ſtone,
No partial love this genuine picture draws,
No venal pencil proſtitutes applauſe:
Juſtice and truth in artleſs colours paint
The Man, the Friend, the Preacher, and the Saint.

VISIONS

IN

VERSE,

FOR THE

ENTERTAINMENT AND INSTRUCTION

OF

YOUNGER MINDS.

Virginibus puerisque canto.   Hor.

Vol. I.   K

CONTAINING,

EPISTLE TO THE READER.

Vision	I.	SLANDER.
	II.	PLEASURE.
	III.	HEALTH.
	IV.	CONTENT.
	V.	HAPPINESS.
	VI.	FRIENDSHIP.
	VII.	MARRIAGE.
	VIII.	LIFE.
	the laſt.	DEATH.

AN EPISTLE TO THE READER.

AUTHORS, you know, of greateſt fame,
Thro' modeſty ſuppreſs their name;
And would you wiſh me to reveal
What theſe ſuperior wits conceal?
Forego the ſearch, my curious friend,
And huſband time to better end.
All my ambition is, I own,
To profit and to pleaſe unknown;
Like ſtreams ſupply'd from ſprings below,
Which ſcatter bleſſings as they flow.
  Were you diſeas'd, or preſs'd with pain,
Strait you'd apply to * Warwick-Lane;

---
* College of Phyſicians.

The thoughtful doctor feels your pulse,
(No matter whether Mead or Hulse)
Writes—Arabic to you and me,—
Then signs his hand, and takes his fee.
Now, should the sage omit his name,
Wou'd not the cure remain the same?
Not but physicians sign their bill,
Or when they cure, or when they kill.

  'Tis often known the mental race
Their fond ambitious fires disgrace.
Dar'd I avow a parent's claim,
Critics might sneer, and friends might blame.
This dang'rous secret let me hide,
I'll tell you every thing beside.
Not that it boots the world a tittle,
Whether the Author's big or little;
Or whether fair, or black, or brown;
No writer's hue concerns the town.

  I pass the silent rural hour,
No slave to wealth, no tool to pow'r.
My mansion's warm, and very neat;
You'd say, a pretty snug retreat.

My rooms no coftly paintings grace,
The humbler print fupplies their place.
Behind the houfe my garden lies,
And opens to the fouthern fkies:
The diftant hills gay profpects yield,
And plenty fmiles in ev'ry field.

   The faithful maftiff is my guard,
The feather'd tribes adorn my yard;
Alive my joy, my treat when dead,
And their foft plumes improve my bed.

   My cow rewards me all fhe can,
(Brutes leave ingratitude to man;)
She, daily thankful to her lord,
Crowns with nectareous fweets my board.
Am I difeas'd?—the cure is known,
Her fweeter juices mend my own.

   I love my houfe, and feldom roam,
Few vifits pleafe me more than home.
I pity that unhappy elf
Who loves all company but felf,
By idle paffions borne away
To op'ra, mafquerade, or play;

Fond of those hives where Folly reigns,
And Britain's peers receive her chains;
Where the pert virgin flights a name,
And scorns to redden into shame.
But know, my fair (to whom belong
The poet and his artless song)
When female cheeks refuse to glow,
Farewell to virtue here below.
Our sex is lost to every rule,
Our sole distinction, Knave or Fool.
'Tis to your innocence we run;
Save us, ye fair, or we're undone;
Maintain your modesty and station,
So Women shall preserve the nation.

 Mothers, 'tis said, in days of old
Esteem'd their girls more choice than gold:
Too well a daughter's worth they knew,
To make her cheap by public view:
(Few, who their diamonds' value weigh,
Expose those diamonds ev'ry day)
Then, if Sir Plume drew near, and smil'd,
The parent trembled for her child:

The

The firſt advance alarm'd her breaſt;
And fancy pictur'd all the reſt.
But now no mother fears a foe,
No daughter ſhudders at a beau.

Pleaſure is all the reigning theme,
Our noon-day thought, our midnight dream.
In Folly's chace our youths engage,
And ſhameleſs crowds of tott'ring age.
The die, the dance, th' intemp'rate bowl
With various charms engroſs the ſoul.
Are gold, fame, health, the terms of vice?
The frantic tribes ſhall pay the price.
But tho' to ruin poſt they run,
They'll think it hard to be undone.

Do not arraign my want of taſte,
Or ſight to ken where joys are plac'd.
They widely err, who think me blind,
And I diſclaim a ſtoic's mind.
Like yours are my ſenſations quite;
I only ſtrive to feel aright.
My joys, like ſtreams, glide gently by,
Tho' ſmall their channel, never dry;

Keep a still, even, fruitful wave,
And bless the neighb'ring meads they lave.
　My fortune (for I'll mention all,
And more than you dare tell) is small;
Yet ev'ry friend partakes my store,
And Want goes smiling from my door.
Will forty shillings warm the breast
Of worth or industry distress'd?
This sum I chearfully impart;
'Tis fourscore pleasures to my heart.
And you may make, by means like these,
Five talents ten, whene'er you please.
'Tis true, my little purse grows light;
But then I sleep so sweet at night!
This grand specific will prevail,
When all the doctor's opiates fail.
　You ask, what party I pursue?
Perhaps you mean, " Whose fool are you?"
The names of party I detest,
Badges of slavery at best!
I've too much grace to play the knave,
And too much pride to turn a slave.

　　　　　　　　　　I love

I love my country from my soul,
And grieve when knaves or fools controul.
I'm pleas'd, when vice and folly smart,
Or at the gibbet or the cart:
Yet always pity, where I can,
Abhor the guilt, but mourn the man.
　Now the religion of your poet—
Does not this little preface show it?
My Visions if you scan with care,
'Tis ten to one you'll find it there.
And if my actions suit my song,
You can't in conscience think me wrong.

SLANDER.

SLANDER.

VISION I.

Inscribed to Miss ****.

MY lovely girl, I write for you;
And pray believe my Visions true;
They'll form your mind to every grace;
They'll add new beauties to your face:
And when old age impairs your prime,
You'll triumph o'er the spoils of time.

Childhood and Youth engage my pen,
'Tis labour lost to talk to Men.
Youth may, perhaps, reform, when wrong,
Age will not listen to my song.
He who at fifty is a fool,
Is far too stubborn grown for school.

What is that vice which still prevails,
When almost every passion fails;
Which with our very dawn begun,
Nor ends, but with our setting sun;

VISION I.

Which, like a noxious weed, can spoil
The fairest flow'rs, and choak the soil?
'Tis Slander,—and, with shame I own,
The vice of human kind alone.

 Be Slander then my leading dream,
Tho' you're a stranger to the theme;
Thy softer breast, and honest heart,
Scorn the defamatory art;
Thy soul asserts her native skies,
Nor asks Detraction's wings to rise;
In foreign spoils let others shine,
Intrinsic excellence is thine.
The bird, in peacock's plumes who shone,
Could plead no merit of her own:
The silly theft betray'd her pride,
And spoke her poverty beside.

 Th' insidious sland'ring thief is worse
Than the poor rogue who steals your purse.
Say, he purloins your glitt'ring store;
Who takes your gold, takes 'trash'—no more;
Perhaps he pilfers—to be fed—
Ah! guiltless wretch, who steals for bread!

         But

But the dark villain, who shall aim
To blast, my fair, thy spotless name,
He'd steal a precious gem away,
Steal what both Indies can't repay!
Here the strong pleas of want are vain,
Or the more impious pleas of gain.
No sinking family to save!
No gold to glut th' insatiate knave!

 Improve the hint of Shakespeare's tongue,
'Twas thus immortal * Shakespeare sung.
And trust the bard's unerring rule,
For Nature was that poet's school.

 As I was nodding in my chair,
I saw a rueful wild appear:
No verdure met my aching sight,
But hemlock, and cold aconite;
Two very pois'nous plants, 'tis true,
But not so bad as vice to you.

 The dreary prospect spread around!
Deep snow had whiten'd all the ground!

* Othello.

A black

VISION I.

A black and barren mountain nigh,
Expos'd to ev'ry friendless sky!
Here foul-mouth'd Slander lay reclin'd,
Her snaky tresses hiss'd behind:
" * A bloated toad-stool rais'd her head,
" The plumes of ravens were her bed:"
She fed upon the viper's brood,
And slak'd her impious thirst with blood.

 The rising sun and western ray
Were witness to her distant sway.
The tyrant claim'd a mightier host
Than the proud Persian e'er could boast.
No conquest grac'd Darius' son †;
By his own numbers half undone!
Success attended Slander's pow'r,
She reap'd fresh laurels ev'ry hour.

* Garth's Dispensary.

† Xerxes, king of Persia, and son of Darius. He invaded Greece with an army consisting of more than a million of men (some say more than two millions) who, together with their cattle, perished in great measure through the inability of the countries to supply such a vast host with provision.

Her

SLANDER.

Her troops a deeper scarlet wore
Than ever armies knew before.
　No plea diverts the fury's rage,
The fury spares nor sex nor age.
Ev'n merit, with destructive charms,
Provokes the vengeance of her arms.
　Whene'er the tyrant sounds to war,
Her canker'd trump is heard afar.
Pride, with a heart unknown to yield,
Commands in chief, and guides the field.
He stalks with vast gigantic stride,
And scatters fear and ruin wide.
So th' impetuous torrents sweep
At once whole nations to the deep.
　Revenge, that base * Hesperian, known
A chief support of Slander's throne,
Amidst the bloody crowd is seen,
And treach'ry brooding in his mien;
The monster often chang'd his gait,
But march'd resolv'd and fix'd as fate.

* Hesperia includes Italy as well as Spain, and the inhabitants of both are remarkable for their revengeful disposition.

Thus

Thus the fell kite, whom hunger stings,
Now slowly moves his outstretch'd wings;
Now swift as lightning bears away,
And darts upon his trembling prey.

Envy commands a secret band,
With sword and poison in her hand.
Around her haggard eye-balls roll;
A thousand fiends possess her soul.
The artful, unsuspected spright
With fatal aim attacks by night.
Her troops advance with silent tread,
And stab the hero in his bed;
Or shoot the wing'd malignant lie,
And female honours pine and die.
So prowling wolves, when darkness reigns,
Intent on murder scour the plains;
Approach the folds, where lambs repose,
Whose guileless breasts suspect no foes;
The savage gluts his fierce desires,
And bleating innocence expires.

Slander smil'd horribly, to view
How wide her daily conquests grew:

Around

Around the crowded levees wait,
Like oriental slaves of state:
Of either sex whole armies press'd,
But chiefly of the fair and best.

Is it a breach of friendship's law
To say what female friends I saw?
Slander assumes the idol's part,
And claims the tribute of the heart.
The best, in some unguarded hour,
Have bow'd the knee, and own'd her pow'r.
Then let the poet not reveal
What candour wishes to conceal.

If I beheld some faulty fair,
Much worse delinquents crowded there:
Prelates in sacred lawn I saw,
Grave physic, and loquacious law;
Courtiers, like summer flies, abound;
And hungry poets swarm around.
But now my partial story ends,
And makes my females full amends.

If Albion's isle such dreams fulfils,
'Tis Albion's isle which cures these ills;

Fertile

VISION I.

Fertile of every worth and grace,
Which warm the heart, and flush the face.

 Fancy disclos'd a smiling train
Of British nymphs, that tripp'd the plain:
Good-nature first, a sylvan queen,
Attir'd in robes of chearful green:
A fair and smiling virgin she!
With ev'ry charm that shines in thee.
Prudence assum'd the chief command,
And bore a mirrour in her hand;
Grey was the matron's head by age,
Her mind by long experience sage;
Of every distant ill afraid,
And anxious for the simp'ring maid.
The Graces danc'd before the fair;
And white-rob'd Innocence was there.
The trees with golden fruits were crown'd,
And rising flow'rs adorn'd the ground;
The sun display'd each brighter ray,
And shone in all the pride of day.
 When Slander sicken'd at the sight,
And skulk'd away to shun the light.

PLEASURE.

VISION II.

HEAR, ye fair mothers of our isle,
Nor scorn your poet's homely style.
What tho' my thoughts be quaint or new,
I'll warrant that my doctrine's true:
Or if my sentiments be old,
Remember, truth is sterling gold.

You judge it of important weight,
To keep your rising offspring strait:
For this such anxious moments feel,
And ask the friendly aids of steel:
For this import the distant cane,
Or slay the monarch of the main.
And shall the soul be warp'd aside
By passion, prejudice, and pride?
Deformity of heart I call
The worst deformity of all.
Your cares to Body are confin'd,
Few fear obliquity of Mind.

Why

VISION II. 147

Why not adorn the better part?
This is a nobler theme for art.
For what is form, or what is face,
But the foul's index, or its cafe?

  Now take a fimile at hand,
Compare the mental foil to land.
Shall fields be till'd with annual care,
And minds lie fallow ev'ry year?
O fince the crop depends on you,
Give them the culture which is due:
Hoe every weed, and drefs the foil,
So harveft fhall repay your toil.

  If human minds refemble trees,
(As every moralift agrees)
Prune all the ftragglers of your vine,
Then fhall the purple clufters fhine.
The gard'ner knows, that fruitful life
Demands his falutary knife:
For ev'ry wild luxuriant fhoot,
Or robs the bloom, or ftarves the fruit.

  A * fatirift in Roman times,
When Rome, like Britain, groan'd with crimes,

* Perfius.

Afferts it for a facred truth,
That Pleafures are the bane of youth:
That forrows fuch purfuits attend,
Or fuch purfuits in forrows end:
That all the wild advent'rer gains
Are perils, penitence, and pains.

 Approve, ye fair, the Roman page,
And bid your fons revere the fage;
In ftudy fpend their midnight oil,
And ftring their nerves by manly toil.
Thus fhall they grow like Temple wife,
Thus future Lockes and Newtons rife;
Or hardy chiefs to wield the lance,
And fave us from the chains of France.
Yes, bid your fons betimes forego
Thofe treach'rous paths were Pleafures grow;
Where the young mind is Folly's flave,
Where every virtue finds a grave.

 Let each bright character be nam'd,
For wifdom or for valour fam'd:
Are the dear youths to fcience prone?
Tell, how th' immortal Bacon fhone!

VISION II.

Who, leaving meaner joys to kings,
Soar'd high on contemplation's wings;
Rang'd the fair fields of nature o'er,
Where never mortal trod before:
Bacon! whose vast capacious plan
Bespoke him angel, more than man!

Does love of martial fame inspire?
Cherish, ye fair, the gen'rous fire;
Teach them to spurn inglorious rest,
And rouse the hero in their breast;
Paint Cressy's vanquish'd field anew,
Their souls shall kindle at the view;
Resolv'd to conquer or to fall,
When Liberty and Britain call.
Thus shall they rule the crimson plain,
Or hurl their thunders thro' the main;
Gain with their blood, nor grudge the cost,
What their degen'rate sires have lost:
The laurel thus shall grace their brow,
As Churchill's once, or Warren's now.

One summer's evening as I stray'd
Along the silent moon-light glade,

With thefe reflections in my breaſt,
Beneath an oak I ſunk to reſt;
A gentle ſlumber intervenes,
And fancy dreſs'd inſtructive ſcenes.

Methought a ſpacious road I 'ſpy'd,
And ſtately trees adorn'd its ſide;
Frequented by a giddy crowd
Of thoughtleſs mortals, vain and loud;
Who tripp'd with jocund heel along,
And bade me join their ſmiling throng.

I ſtrait obey'd—Perſuaſion hung
Like honey on the ſpeaker's tongue.
A cloudleſs ſun improv'd the day,
And pinks and roſes ſtrew'd our way.

Now as our journey we purſue,
A beauteous fabric roſe to view,
A ſtately dome, and ſweetly grac'd
With ev'ry ornament of taſte.
This ſtructure was a female's claim,
And Pleaſure was the monarch's name.

The hall we enter'd uncontroul'd,
And ſaw the queen enthron'd on gold;

Arabian

VISION II.

Arabian sweets perfum'd the ground,
And laughing Cupids flutter'd round;
A flowing vest adorn'd the fair,
And flow'ry chaplets wreath'd her hair:
Fraud taught the queen a thousand wiles,
A thousand soft insidious smiles;
Love taught her lisping tongue to speak,
And form'd the dimple in her cheek;
The lily and the damask rose,
The tincture of her face compose;
Nor did the god of Wit disdain
To mingle with the shining train.

 Her vot'ries flock from various parts,
And chiefly youth resign'd their hearts;
The old in sparing numbers press'd,
But awkward devotees at best.

 Now let us range at large, we cry'd,
Thro' all the garden's boasted pride.
Here jasmines spread the silver flow'r,
To deck the wall, or weave the bow'r;
The woodbines mix in am'rous play,
And breathe their fragrant lives away.

Here rising myrtles form a shade,
There roses blush, and scent the glade.
The orange, with a vernal face,
Wears ev'ry rich autumnal grace;
While the young blossoms here unfold,
There shines the fruit like pendent gold.
Citrons their balmy sweets exhale,
And triumph in the distant gale.
Now fountains, murm'ring to the song,
Roll their translucent streams along.
Thro' all the aromatic groves,
The faithful turtles coo their loves.
The lark ascending pours his notes,
And linnets swell their rapt'rous throats.

Pleasure, imperial fair! how gay
Thy empire, and how wide thy sway!
Enchanting queen! how soft thy reign!
How man, fond man! implores thy chain!
Yet thine each meretricious art,
That weakens, and corrupts the heart.
The childish toys and wanton page
Which sink and prostitute the stage!

The

The masquerade, that just offence
To virtue, and reproach to sense!
The midnight dance, the mantling bowl,
And all that dissipate the soul;
All that to ruin man combine,
Yes, specious harlot, all are thine!

 Whence sprung th' accursed lust of play,
Which beggars thousands in a day?
Speak, sorc'ress, speak (for thou canst tell)
Who call'd the treach'rous card from hell?
Now man profanes his reas'ning pow'rs,
Profanes sweet friendship's sacred hours;
Abandon'd to inglorious ends,
And faithless to himself and friends;
A dupe to ev'ry artful knave,
To ev'ry abject wish a slave;
But who against himself combines,
Abets his enemy's designs.
When Rapine meditates a blow,
He shares the guilt who aids the foe.
Is man a thief who steals my pelf?
How great his theft, who robs himself!

PLEASURE.

Is man, who gulls his friend, a cheat?
How heinous then is self-deceit!
Is murder justly deem'd a crime?
How black his guilt, who murders time!
Shou'd custom plead, as custom will,
Grand precedents to palliate ill,
Shall modes and forms avail with me,
When Reason disavows the plea?
Who games, is felon of his wealth,
His time, his liberty, his health.
Virtue forsakes his sordid mind,
And Honour scorns to stay behind.
From man when these bright cherubs part,
Ah! what's the poor deserted heart?
A savage wild that shocks the sight,
Or chaos, and impervious night!
Each gen'rous principle destroy'd,
And dæmons crowd the frightful void!

 Shall Siam's elephant supply
The baneful desolating die?
Against the honest sylvan's will,
You taught his iv'ry tusk to kill.

Heav'n, fond its favours to difpenfe,
Gave him that weapon for defence.
That weapon, for his guard defign'd,
You render'd fatal to mankind.
He plann'd no death for thoughtlefs youth,
You gave the venom to his tooth.
Blufh, tyrant, blufh, for oh! 'tis true
That no fell ferpent bites like you.

 The guefts were order'd to depart,
Reluctance fat on ev'ry heart:
A porter fhew'd a different door,
Not the fair portal known before!
The gates, methought, were open'd wide,
The crowds defcended in a tide.
But oh! ye heav'ns, what vaft furprize
Struck the advent'rers' frighted eyes!
A barren heath before us lay,
And gath'ring clouds obfcur'd the day;
The darknefs rofe in fmoky fpires;
The lightnings flafh'd their livid fires:
Loud peals of thunder rent the air,
While Vengeance chill'd our hearts with fear.

Five

Five ruthless tyrants sway'd the plain,
And triumph'd o'er the mangled slain.
Here sat Distaste, with sickly mien,
And more than half-devour'd with spleen:
There stood Remorse, with thought opprest,
And vipers feeding on his breast:
Then Want, dejected, pale, and thin,
With bones just starting thro' his skin;
A ghastly fiend!—and close behind
Disease, his aching head reclin'd!
His everlasting thirst confess'd
The fires, which rag'd within his breast:
Death clos'd the train! the hideous form
Smil'd unrelenting in the storm:
When strait a doleful shriek was heard;
I 'woke—The vision disappear'd.

Let not the unexperienc'd boy
Deny that Pleasures will destroy;
Or say that dreams are vain and wild,
Like fairy tales, to please a child.
Important hints the wise may reap
From sallies of the soul in sleep.

And,

And, since there's meaning in my dream,
The moral merits your esteem.

HEALTH.

VISION III.

ATTEND my Visions, thoughtless youths,
Ere long you'll think them weighty truths;
Prudent it were to think so now;
Ere age has silver'd o'er your brow:
For he, who at his early years
Has sown in vice, shall reap in tears.
If folly has possess'd his prime,
Disease shall gather strength in time;
Poison shall rage in ev'ry vein,—
Nor penitence dilute the stain:
And when each hour shall urge his fate,
Thought, like the doctor, comes too late.

   The subject of my song is Health,
A good superior far to wealth.

Can the young mind distrust its worth?
Consult the monarchs of the earth:
Imperial czars, and sultans, own
No gem so bright, that decks their throne:
Each for this pearl his crown would quit,
And turn a rustic, or a cit.

   Mark, tho' the blessing's lost with ease,
'Tis not recover'd when you please.
Say not that gruels shall avail,
For salutary gruels fail.
Say not, Apollo's sons succeed,
Apollo's son is Egypt's * reed.
How fruitless the physician's skill,
How vain the penitential pill,
The marble monuments proclaim,
The humbler turf confirms the same!
Prevention is the better cure,
So says the proverb, and 'tis sure.

   Would you extend your narrow span,
And make the most of life you can;

* In allusion to 2 Kings xviii. 21.

VISION III.

Would you, when med'cines cannot save,
Descend with ease into the grave;
Calmly retire, like evening light,
And chearful bid the world good-night?
Let temp'rance constantly preside,
Our best physician, friend, and guide!
Would you to wisdom make pretence,
Proud to be thought a man of sense?
Let temp'rance (always friend to fame)
With steady hand direct your aim;
Or, like an archer in the dark,
Your random shaft will miss the mark:
For they who slight her golden rules,
In wisdom's volume stand for fools.

But morals, unadorn'd by art,
Are seldom known to reach the heart.
I'll therefore strive to raise my theme
With all the scenery of dream.

Soft were my slumbers, sweet my rest,
Such as the infant's on the breast;
When Fancy, ever on the wing,
And fruitful as the genial spring,

Presented, in a blaze of light,
A new creation to my sight.

A rural landscape I descry'd,
Drest in the robes of summer pride;
The herds adorn'd the sloping hills,
That glitter'd with their tinkling rills;
Below the fleecy mothers stray'd,
And round their sportive lambkins play'd.

Nigh to a murmuring brook I saw
An humble cottage thatch'd with straw;
Behind, a garden that supply'd
All things for use, and none for pride:
Beauty prevail'd thro' ev'ry part,
But more of nature than of art.

Hail, thou sweet, calm, unenvied seat!
I said, and bless'd the fair retreat:
Here would I pass my remnant days,
Unknown to censure, or to praise;
Forget the world, and be forgot,
As Pope describes his vestal's lot.

While thus I mus'd, a beauteous maid
Stept from a thicket's neighb'ring shade;

Not

Not Hampton's gallery can boaſt,
Nor Hudſon paint ſo fair a toaſt:
She claim'd the cottage for her own,
To Health a cottage is a throne.

   The annals ſay (to prove her worth)
The Graces ſolemniz'd her birth.
Garlands of various flow'rs they wrought,
The orchard's bluſhing pride they brought:
Hence in her face the lily ſpeaks,
And hence the roſe which paints her cheeks;
The cherry gave her lips to glow,
Her eyes were debtors to the ſloe;
And, to compleat the lovely fair,
'Tis ſaid, the cheſnut ſtain'd her hair.

   The virgin was averſe to courts,
But often ſeen in rural ſports:
When in her roſy veſt the morn
Walks o'er the dew-beſpangled lawn,
The nymph is firſt to form the race,
Or wind the horn, and lead the chace.

   Sudden I heard a ſhouting train,
Glad acclamations fill'd the plain:

Unbounded joy improv'd the scene,
For Health was loud proclaim'd a queen.
 Two smiling cherubs grac'd her throne,
(To modern courts, I fear, unknown;)
One was the nymph, that loves the light,
Fair Innocence, array'd in white;
With sister Peace in close embrace,
And heav'n all opening in her face.
 The reign was long, the empire great,
And Virtue, minister of state.
In other kingdoms, ev'ry hour,
You hear of vice preferr'd to pow'r:
Vice was a perfect stranger here:
No knaves engross'd the royal ear:
No fools obtain'd this monarch's grace;
Virtue dispos'd of ev'ry place.
 What sickly appetites are ours,
Still varying with the varying hours!
And tho' from good to bad we range,
" No matter," says the fool, " 'tis change."
 Her subjects now express'd apace
Dissatisfaction in their face:

VISION III.

Some view the state with envy's eye,
Some were displeas'd, they knew not why:
When Faction, ever bold and vain,
With rigour tax'd their monarch's reign.
Thus, should an angel from above,
Fraught with benevolence and love,
Descend to earth, and here impart
Important truths to mend the heart;
Would not th' instructive guest dispense
With passion, appetite, and sense,
We should his heav'nly lore despise,
And send him to his former skies.

A dang'rous hostile power arose
To Health, whose houshold were her foes:
A harlot's loose attire she wore,
And Luxury the name she bore.
This princess of unbounded sway,
Whom Asia's softer sons obey,
Made war against the queen of Health,
Assisted by the troops of Wealth.

The queen was first to take the field,
Arm'd with her helmet and her shield;

Temper'd with such superior art,
That both were proof to ev'ry dart.
Two warlike chiefs approach'd the green,
And wondrous fav'rites with the queen:
Both were of Amazonian race,
Both high in merit, and in place.
Here, Resolution march'd, whose soul
No fear could shake, no pow'r controul;
The heroine wore a Roman vest,
A lion's heart inform'd her breast.
There Prudence shone, whose bosom wrought
With all the various plans of thought;
'Twas her's to bid the troops engage,
And teach the battle where to rage.

And now the Siren's armies press,
Their van was headed by Excess:
The mighty wings, that form'd the side,
Commanded by that giant Pride:
While Sickness, and her sisters Pain
And Poverty, the centre gain:
Repentance, with a brow severe,
And Death, were station'd in the rear.

Health

Health rang'd her troops with matchless art,
And acted the defensive part:
Her army posted on a hill,
Plainly bespoke superior skill:
Hence were discover'd thro' the plain,
The motions of the hostile train:
While Prudence, to prevent surprize,
Oft sally'd with her trusty spies;
Explor'd each ambuscade below,
And reconnoitred well the foe.

   Afar when Luxury descry'd
Inferior force by art supply'd,
The Siren spake—Let fraud prevail,
Since all my numerous hosts must fail;
Henceforth hostilities shall cease,
I'll send to Health and offer peace.
Strait she dispatch'd, with pow'rs compleat,
Pleasure, her minister, to treat.
This wicked strumpet topp'd her part,
And sow'd sedition in the heart!
Thro' ev'ry troop the poison ran,
All were infected to a man.

The wary generals were won
By Pleasure's wiles, and both undone.
   Jove held the troops in high disgrace,
And bade diseases blast their race;
Look'd on the queen with melting eyes,
And snatch'd his darling to the skies:
Who still regards those wiser few,
That dare her dictates to pursue.
For where her stricter law prevails,
Tho' Passion prompts, or Vice assails;
Long shall the cloudless skies behold,
And their calm sun-set beam with gold.

CONTENT.

VISION IV.

MAN is deceiv'd by outward show—
'Tis a plain homespun truth, I know,
The fraud prevails at ev'ry age,
So says the school-boy and the sage;

Yet

Yet still we hug the dear deceit,
And still exclaim against the cheat.
But whence this inconsistent part?
Say, moralists, who know the heart:
If you'll this labyrinth pursue,
I'll go before, and find the clue.

   I dreamt ('twas on a birth-day night)
A sumptuous palace rose to sight;
The builder had, thro' ev'ry part,
Observ'd the chastest rules of art;
Raphael and Titian had display'd
All the full force of light and shade:
Around the livery'd servants wait;
An aged porter kept the gate.

   As I was traversing the hall,
Where Brussels' looms adorn'd the wall,
(Whose tap'stry shews, without my aid,
A nun is no such useless maid)
A graceful person came in view
(His form, it seems, is known to few;)
His dress was unadorn'd with lace,
But charms! a thousand in his face.

This, sir, your property? I cry'd—
Master and mansion coincide:
Where all, indeed, is truly great,
And proves, that bliss may dwell with state.
Pray, sir, indulge a stranger's claim,
And grant the favour of your name.

" Content," the lovely form reply'd;
But think not here that I reside:
Here lives a courtier, base and sly;
An open, honest rustic, I.
Our taste and manners disagree,
His levee boasts no charms for me:
For titles, and the smiles of kings,
To me are cheap unheeded things.
('Tis virtue can alone impart
The patent of a ducal heart:
Unless this herald speaks him great,
What shall avail the glare of state?)
Those secret charms are my delight,
Which shine remote from public sight:
Passions subdu'd, desires at rest—
And hence his chaplain shares my breast.

There

VISION IV.

    There was a time (his grace can tell)
I knew the duke exceeding well;
Knew ev'ry secret of his heart;
In truth, we never were apart:
But when the court became his end,
He turn'd his back upon his friend.

    One day I call'd upon his grace,
Just as the duke had got a place:
I thought (but thought amiss, 'tis clear)
I shou'd be welcome to the peer,
Yes, welcome to a man in pow'r;
And so I was—for half an hour.
But he grew weary of his guest,
And soon discarded me his breast;
Upbraided me with want of merit,
But most for poverty of spirit.

    You relish not the great man's lot?
Come, hasten to my humbler cot.
Think me not partial to the great,
I'm a sworn foe to pride and state;
No monarchs share my kind embrace,
There's scarce a monarch knows my face:

                             Content

CONTENT.

Content shuns courts, and oft'ner dwells
With modest worth in rural cells;
There's no complaint, tho' brown the bread,
Or the rude turf sustain the head;
Tho' hard the couch, and coarse the meat,
Still the brown loaf and sleep are sweet.

 Far from the city I reside,
And a thatch'd cottage all my pride.
True to my heart, I seldom roam,
Because I find my joys at home:
For foreign visits then begin,
When the man feels a void within.

 But tho' from towns and crowds I fly,
No humorist, nor cynic, I.
Amidst sequester'd shades I prize
The friendships of the good and wise.
Bid Virtue and her sons attend,
Virtue will tell thee I'm her friend:
Tell thee, I'm faithful, constant, kind,
And meek, and lowly, and resign'd;
Will say, there's no distinction known
Betwixt her houshold and my own.

AUTHOR.]

VISION IV.

AUTHOR.] If these the friendships you pursue,
Your friends, I fear, are very few.
So little company, you say,
Yet fond of home from day to day?
How do you shun detraction's rod?
I doubt your neighbours think you odd!

CONTENT.] I commune with myself at night,
And ask my heart if all be right:
If, "Right," replies my faithful breast,
I smile, and close my eyes to rest.

AUTHOR.] You seem regardless of the town:
Pray, sir, how stand you with the gown?

CONTENT.] The clergy say they love me well,
Whether they do, they best can tell:
They paint me modest, friendly, wise,
And always praise me to the skies;
But if conviction's at the heart,
Why not a correspondent part?
For shall the learned tongue prevail,
If actions preach a different tale?
Who'll seek my door or grace my walls,
When neither dean nor prelate calls?

With thofe my friendfhips moft obtain,
Who prize their duty more than gain;
Soft flow the hours whene'er we meet,
And confcious virtue is our treat;
Our harmlefs breafts no envy know,
And hence we fear no fecret foe;
Our walks Ambition ne'er attends,
And hence we afk no powerful friends;
We wifh the beft to church and ftate,
But leave the fteerage to the great;
Carelefs, who rifes, or who falls,
And never dream of vacant ftalls;
Much lefs, by pride or int'reft drawn,
Sigh for the mitre, and the lawn.

 Obferve the fecrets of my art,
I'll fundamental truths impart:
If you'll my kind advice purfue,
I'll quit my hut, and dwell with you.

 The paffions are a num'rous crowd,
Imperious, pofitive, and loud:
Curb thefe licentious fons of ftrife;
Hence chiefly rife the ftorms of life:

VISION IV.

If they grow mutinous, and rave,
They are thy masters, thou their slave.
  Regard the world with cautious eye,
Nor raise your expectation high.
See that the balanc'd scales be such,
You neither fear nor hope too much.
For disappointment's not the thing,
'Tis pride and passion point the sting,
Life is a sea where storms must rise,
'Tis Folly talks of cloudless skies:
He who contracts his swelling sail,
Eludes the fury of the gale.
  Be still, nor anxious thoughts employ,
Distrust embitters present joy:
On God for all events depend;
You cannot want when God's your friend,
Weigh well your part, and do your best;
Leave to your Maker all the rest.
The hand which form'd thee in the womb,
Guides from the cradle to the tomb.
Can the fond mother slight her boy;
Can she forget her prattling joy?

Say

Say then, shall Sov'reign Love desert
The humble, and the honest heart?
Heav'n may not grant thee all thy mind;
Yet say not thou that Heav'n's unkind.
God is alike, both good and wise,
In what he grants, and what denies:
Perhaps, what goodness gives to-day,
To-morrow goodness takes away.

 You say, that troubles intervene,
That sorrows darken half the scene.
True—and this consequence you see,
The world was ne'er design'd for thee:
You're like a passenger below,
That stays perhaps a night or so;
But still his native country lies
Beyond the bound'ries of the skies.

 Of Heav'n ask virtue, wisdom, health,
But never let thy pray'r be wealth.
If food be thine, (tho' little gold)
And raiment to repel the cold;
Such as may nature's wants suffice,
Not what from pride and folly rise;

VISION IV.

If soft the motions of thy soul,
And a calm confcience crowns the whole;
Add but a friend to all this ftore,
You can't in reafon wifh for more:
And if kind Heav'n this comfort brings,
'Tis more than Heav'n beftows on kings.

 He fpake—the airy fpectre flies,
And ftrait the fweet illufion dies.
The vifion, at the early dawn,
Confign'd me to the thoughtful morn;
To all the cares of waking clay,
And inconfiftent dreams of day.

HAPPINESS.

HAPPINESS.

VISION V.

YE ductile youths, whose rising sun
   Hath many circles still to run;
Who wisely wish the pilot's chart,
To steer thro' life th' unsteady heart;
And all the thoughtful voyage past,
To gain a happy port at last:
Attend a Seer's instructive song,
For moral truths to dreams belong.

  I saw this wondrous vision soon,
Long ere my sun had reach'd its noon;
Just when the rising beard began
To grace my chin, and call me man.

  One night, when balmy slumbers shed
Their peaceful poppies o'er my head,
My fancy led me to explore
A thousand scenes unknown before.

                        I saw

VISION V.

I saw a plain extended wide,
And crowds pour'd in from ev'ry side:
All seem'd to start a diff'rent game,
Yet all declar'd their views the same:
The chace was Happiness, I found,
But all, alas! enchanted ground.

 Indeed I judg'd it wondrous strange,
To see the giddy numbers range
Thro' roads, which promis'd nought, at best,
But sorrow to the human breast.
Methought, if bliss was all their view,
Why did they diff'rent paths pursue?
The waking world has long agreed,
That Bagshot's not the road to Tweed:
And he who Berwick seeks thro' Staines,
Shall have his labour for his pains.

 As Parnel * says, my bosom wrought
With travail of uncertain thought:
And, as an angel help'd the dean,
My angel chose to intervene;
The dress of each was much the same,
And Virtue was my seraph's name.

    * The Hermit.

When thus the angel silence broke,
(Her voice was music as she spoke.)
  Attend, O man, nor leave my side,
And safety shall thy footsteps guide;
Such truths I'll teach, such secrets show,
As none but favour'd mortals know.
  She said—and strait we march'd along
To join Ambition's active throng:
Crowds urg'd on crowds with eager pace,
And happy he who led the race.
Axes and daggers lay unseen
In ambuscade along the green;
While vapours shed delusive light,
And bubbles mock'd the distant fight.
  We saw a shining mountain rise,
Whose tow'ring summit reach'd the skies:
The slopes were steep, and form'd of glass,
Painful and hazardous to pass:
Courtiers and statesmen led the way,
The faithless paths their steps betray;
This moment seen aloft to soar,
The next to fall and rise no more.

'Twas

VISION V.

'Twas here Ambition kept her court,
A phantom of gigantic port;
The fav'rite that suſtain'd her throne,
Was Falſchood, by her vizard known;
Next ſtood Miſtruſt, with frequent ſigh,
Diſorder'd look, and ſquinting eye;
While meagre Envy claim'd a place,
And Jealouſy with jaundic'd face.
 But where is Happineſs? I cry'd.
My guardian turn'd, and thus reply'd.
 Mortal, by folly ſtill beguil'd,
Thou haſt not yet outſtripp'd the child;
Thou, who haſt twenty winters ſeen,
(I hardly think thee paſt fifteen)
To aſk if Happineſs can dwell
With every dirty imp of hell!
Go to the ſchool-boy, he ſhall preach,
What twenty winters cannot teach;
He'll tell thee, from his weekly theme,
That thy purſuit is all a dream:
That Bliſs ambitious views diſowns,
And ſelf-dependent, laughs at thrones;

Prefers the shades and lowly seats,
Whither fair Innocence retreats:
So the coy lily of the vale,
Shuns eminence, and loves the dale.

 I blush'd; and now we cross'd the plain,
To find the money-getting train;
Those silent, snug, commercial bands,
With busy looks, and dirty hands.
Amidst these thoughtful crowds the old
Plac'd all their Happiness in gold.
And surely, if there's bliss below,
These hoary heads the secret know.

 We journey'd with the plodding crew,
When soon a temple rose to view:
A Gothic pile, with moss o'ergrown;
Strong were the walls, and built with stone.
Without a thousand mastiffs wait:
A thousand bolts secure the gate.
We sought admission long in vain;
For here all favours fell for gain:
The greedy porter yields to gold,
His fee receiv'd, the gates unfold.

VISION V.

Assembled nations here we found,
And view'd the cringing herds around,
Who daily sacrific'd to Wealth,
Their honour, conscience, peace, and health.
I saw no charms that could engage;
The God appear'd like sordid age,
With hooked nose, and famish'd jaws,
But serpents' eyes and harpies' claws:
Behind stood Fear, that restless spright,
Which haunts the watches of the night;
And Viper-Care, that stings so deep,
Whose deadly venom murders sleep.

 We hasten now to Pleasure's bow'rs;
Where the gay tribes sat crown'd with flow'rs:
Here Beauty every charm display'd,
And Love inflam'd the yielding maid:
Delicious Wine our taste employs,
His crimson bowl exalts our joys:
I felt its gen'rous pow'r, and thought
The pearl was found, that long I sought.
Determin'd here to fix my home,
I bless'd the change, nor wish'd to roam:

HAPPINESS.

The Seraph disapprov'd my stay,
Spread her fair plumes, and wing'd away.

Alas! whene'er we talk of bliss,
How prone is man to judge amiss!
See, a long train of ills conspires
To scourge our uncontroul'd desires.
Like summer swarms Diseases crowd,
Each bears a crutch, or each a shroud:
Fever! that thirsty fury, came,
With inextinguishable flame;
Consumption, sworn ally of Death!
Crept slowly on with panting breath;
Gout roar'd, and shew'd his throbbing feet;
And Dropsy took the drunkard's seat:
Stone brought his tort'ring racks; and near
Sat Palsy shaking in her chair!

A mangled youth, beneath a shade,
A melancholy scene display'd:
His noseless face, and loathsome stains,
Proclaim'd the poison in his veins;
He rais'd his eyes, he smote his breast,
He wept aloud, and thus address'd:

       Forbear

VISION V.

Forbear the harlot's false embrace,
Tho' Lewdness wear an angel's face.
Be wise, by my experience taught,
I die, alas! for want of thought.

As he, who travels Lybia's plains,
Where the fierce lion lawless reigns,
Is seiz'd with fear and wild dismay,
When the grim foe obstructs his way:
My soul was pierc'd with equal fright,
My tott'ring limbs oppos'd my flight;
I call'd on Virtue, but in vain,
Her absence quicken'd every pain:
At length the slighted angel heard,
The dear refulgent form appear'd.

Presumptuous youth! she said, and frown'd;
(My heart-strings flutter'd at the sound)
Who turns to me reluctant ears,
Shall shed repeated floods of tears.
These rivers shall for ever last,
There's no retracting what is past:
Nor think avenging ills to shun;
Play a false card, and you're undone.

HAPPINESS.

Of Pleasure's gilded baits beware,
Nor tempt the Syren's fatal snare:
Forego this curs'd, detested place,
Abhor the strumpet, and her race:
Had you those softer paths pursu'd,
Perdition, stripling, had ensu'd:
Yes, fly——you stand upon its brink;
To-morrow is too late to think.

Indeed unwelcome truths I tell,
But mark my sacred lesson well:
With me whoever lives at strife,
Loses his better friend for life;
With me who lives in friendship's ties,
Finds all that's sought for by the wise.
Folly exclaims, and well she may,
Because I take her mask away;
If once I bring her to the sun,
The painted harlot is undone.
But prize, my child, oh! prize my rules,
And leave deception to her fools.

Ambition deals in tinsel toys,
Her traffic gewgaws, fleeting joys!

An

VISION V.

An arrant juggler in disguise,
Who holds false optics to your eyes.
But ah! how quick the shadows pass;
Tho' the bright visions thro' her glass
Charm at a distance; yet, when near,
The baseless fabrics disappear.

   Nor Riches boast intrinsic worth,
Their charms at best, superior earth:
These oft the heav'n-born mind enslave,
And make an honest man a knave.
" Wealth cures my wants," the Miser cries;
Be not deceiv'd—the Miser lies:
One want he has, with all his store,
That worst of wants! the want of more.

   Take Pleasure, Wealth, and Pomp away,
And where is Happiness? you say.

   'Tis here—and may be yours—for, know
I'm all that's Happiness below.

   To Vice I leave tumultuous joys,
Mine is the still and softer voice;
That whispers peace, when storms invade,
And music thro' the midnight shade.

                       Come

Come then, be mine in ev'ry part,
Nor give me less, than all your heart;
When troubles discompose your breast,
I'll enter there a chearful guest:
My converse shall your cares beguile,
The little world within shall smile;
And then it scarce imports a jot,
Whether the great world frowns or not.
  And when the closing scenes prevail,
When wealth, state, pleasure, all shall fail;
All that a foolish world admires,
Or passion craves, or pride inspires;
At that important hour of need,
Virtue shall prove a friend indeed!
My hands shall smooth thy dying bed,
My arms sustain thy drooping head:
And when the painful struggle's o'er,
And that vain thing, the World, no more;
I'll bear my fav'rite son away
To rapture, and eternal day.

FRIENDSHIP.

FRIENDSHIP.

VISION VI.

FRIENDSHIP! thou soft, propitious pow'r!
Sweet regent of the social hour!
Sublime thy joys, nor understood
But by the virtuous and the good!
Cabal and Riot take thy name,
But 'tis a false affected claim.
In heav'n if Love and Friendship dwell,
Can they associate e'er with hell?
   Thou art the same thro' change of times,
Thro' frozen zones, and burning climes:
From the æquator to the pole,
The same kind angel thro' the whole.
And, since thy choice is always free,
I bless thee for thy smiles on me.
   When sorrows swell the tempest high,
Thou, a kind port, art always nigh;

For aching hearts a fov'reign cure,
Not foft Nepenthe * half fo fure!
And when returning comforts rife,
Thou the bright fun that gilds our fkies.

While thefe ideas warm'd my breaft,
My weary eye-lids ftole to reft;
When Fancy re-affum'd the theme,
And furnifh'd this inftructive dream.

I fail'd upon a ftormy fea,
(Thoufands embark'd alike with me)
My fkiff was fmall, and weak befide,
Not built, methought, to ftem the tide.
The winds along the furges fweep,
The wrecks lie fcatter'd thro' the deep;
Aloud the foaming billows roar,
Unfriendly rocks forbid the fhore.

While all our various courfe purfue,
A fpacious ifle falutes our view.

* Nepenthe is an herb, which being infufed in wine, difpels grief. It is unknown to the moderns; but fome believe it a kind of opium, and others take it for a fpecies of buglofs. Plin. 21. 21f & 25. 2.

Two

VISION VI.

Two queens, with tempers diff'ring wide,
This new-discover'd world divide.
A river parts their proper claim,
And Truth its celebrated name.

   One side a beauteous tract of ground
Presents, with living verdure crown'd.
The seasons temp'rate, soft, and mild,
And a kind sun that always smil'd.

   Few storms molest the natives here;
Cold is the only ill they fear.
This happy clime, and grateful soil,
With plenty crowns the lab'rer's toil.

   Here Friendship's happy kingdom grew,
Her realms were small, her subjects few.
A thousand charms the palace grace,
A rock of adamant its base.
Tho' thunders roll, and lightnings fly,
This structure braves th' inclement sky.
Ev'n Time, which other piles devours,
And mocks the pride of human pow'rs,
Partial to Friendship's pile alone,
Cements the joints, and binds the stone;

                         Ripens

Ripens the beauties of the place;
And calls to life each latent grace.
   Around the throne, in order stand
Four Amazons, a trusty band;
Friends ever faithful to advise,
Or to defend when dangers rise.
Here Fortitude in coat of mail!
There Justice lifts her golden scale!
Two hardy chiefs! who persevere,
With form erect, and brow severe;
Who smile at perils, pains, and death,
And triumph with their latest breath.
   Temp'rance, that comely matron's near,
Guardian of all the Virtues here;
Adorn'd with ev'ry blooming grace,
Without one wrinkle in her face.
   But Prudence most attracts the sight,
And shines pre-eminently bright.
To view her various thoughts that rise,
She holds a mirrour to her eyes;
The mirrour, faithful to its charge,
Reflects the virgin's soul in large.

VISION VI.

A Virtue with a softer air,
Was handmaid to the regal fair.
This nymph, indulgent, constant, kind,
Derives from Heav'n her spotless mind;
When actions wear a dubious face,
Puts the best meaning on the case;
She spreads her arms, and bares her breast,
Takes in the naked and distress'd;
Prefers the hungry orphan's cries,
And from her queen obtains supplies.
The maid, who acts this lovely part,
Grasp'd in her hand a bleeding heart.
Fair Charity! be thou my guest,
And be thy constant couch my breast.

But Virtues of inferior name,
Crowd round the throne with equal claim;
In loyalty by none surpass'd,
They hold allegiance to the last.
Not ancient records e'er can show
That one deserted to the foe.

The river's other side display'd
Alternate plots of flow'rs and shade,

Where

FRIENDSHIP.

Where poppies shone with various hue,
Where yielding willows plenteous grew;
And Humble * plants, by trav'llers thought
With slow but certain poison fraught.
Beyond these scenes, the eye descry'd
A pow'rful realm extended wide,
Whose bound'ries from north-east begun,
And stretch'd to meet the south-west sun.
Here Flatt'ry boasts despotic sway,
And basks in all the warmth of day.
   Long practis'd in Deception's school,
The tyrant knew the arts to rule;
Elated with th' imperial robe,
She plans the conquest of the globe;
And aided by her servile trains,
Leads kings, and sons of kings, in chains.
Her darling minister is Pride,
(Who ne'er was known to change his side)
A friend to all her interests just,
And active to discharge his trust;

---

* The Humble plant bends down before the touch (as the Sensitive plant shrinks from the touch) and is said by some to be the slow poison of the Indians.

VISION VI.

Caress'd alike by high and low,
The idol of the belle and beau:
In ev'ry shape, he shews his skill,
And forms her subjects to his will;
Enters their houses and their hearts,
And gains his point before he parts.
Sure never minister was known
So zealous for his sov'reign's throne!

Three sisters, similar in mien,
Were maids of honour to the queen:
Who farther favours shar'd beside,
As daughters of her statesman Pride.
The first, Conceit, with tow'ring crest,
Who look'd with scorn upon the rest;
Fond of herself, nor less, I deem,
Than duchess in her own esteem.

Next Affectation, fair and young,
With half-form'd accents on her tongue,
Whose antic shapes, and various face,
Distorted every native grace.

Then Vanity, a wanton maid,
Flaunting in Brussels and brocade;

Fantastic,

Fantaſtic, frolicſome, and wild,
With all the trinkets of a child.

The people, loyal to the queen,
Wore their attachment in their mien:
With chearful heart they homage paid,
And happieſt he, who moſt obey'd.
While they, who ſought their own applauſe,
Promoted moſt their ſov'reign's cauſe.
The minds of all were fraught with guile,
Their manners diſſolute and vile;
And every tribe, like Pagans, run
To kneel before the riſing ſun.

But now ſome clam'rous ſounds ariſe,
And all the pleaſing viſion flies.

Once more I clos'd my eyes to ſleep,
And gain'd th' imaginary deep;
Fancy preſided at the helm,
And ſteer'd me back to Friendſhip's realm.
But oh! with horror I relate
The revolutions of her ſtate.
The Trojan chief cou'd hardly more
His Aſiatic tow'rs deplore.

VISION VI.

For Flatt'ry view'd thofe fairer plains,
With longing eyes, where Friendfhip reigns,
With envy heard her neighbour's fame,
And often figh'd to gain the fame.
At length, by pride and int'reft fir'd,
To Friendfhip's kingdom fhe afpir'd.

And now commencing open foe,
She plans in thought fome mighty blow;
Draws out her forces on the green,
And marches to invade the queen.

The river Truth the hofts withftood,
And roll'd her formidable flood:
Her current ftrong, and deep, and clear,
No fords were found, no ferries near:
But as the troops approach'd the waves,
Their fears fuggeft a thoufand graves;
They all retir'd with hafte extreme,
And fhudder'd at the dang'rous ftream.

Hypocrify the gulph explores;
She forms a bridge, and joins the fhores,
Thus often art or fraud prevails,
When military prowefs fails.

The troops an easy paffage find,
And Vict'ry follows clofe behind.
  Friendfhip with ardour charg'd her foes,
And now the fight promifcuous grows;
But Flatt'ry threw a poifon'd dart,
And pierc'd the Emprefs to the heart.
The Virtues all around were feen
To fall in heaps about the queen.
The tyrant ftript the mangled fair,
She wore her fpoils, affum'd her air;
And mounting next the fuff'rer's throne,
Claim'd the queen's titles as her own.
  Ah! injur'd maid, aloud I cry'd,
Ah! injur'd maid, the rocks reply'd:
But judge my griefs, and fhare them too,
For the fad tale pertains to you;
Judge, reader, how fevere the wound,
When Friendfhip's foes were mine, I found;
When the fad fcene of pride and guile
Was Britain's poor degen'rate ifle.
  The Amazons, who propp'd the ftate,
Haply furviv'd the gen'ral fate.
Juftice

Justice to Powis-House is fled,
And Yorke sustains her radiant head.
The virtue Fortitude appears
In open day at Ligonier's;
Illustrious heroine of the sky,
Who leads to vanquish or to die!
'Twas she our vet'rans breasts inspir'd,
When Belgia's faithless sons retir'd:
For Tournay's treach'rous tow'rs can tell
Britannia's children greatly fell.

No partial virtue of the plain!
She rous'd the lions of the main:
Hence * Vernon's little fleet succeeds,
And hence the gen'rous † Cornwall bleeds!
Hence ‡ Greenville glorious!—for she smil'd
On the young hero from a child.

Tho' in high life such virtues dwell,
They'll suit plebeian breasts as well.

* At Porto Bello.
† Against the combined fleets of France and Spain.
‡ Died in a later engagement with the French fleet.

Say, that the mighty and the great
Blaze like meridian suns of state;
Effulgent excellence display,
Like Hallifax, in floods of day;
Our lesser orbs may pour their light,
Like the mild crescent of the night.
Tho' pale our beams, and small our sphere,
Still we may shine serene and clear.

Give to the judge the scarlet gown,
To martial souls the civic crown:
What then? is merit their's alone?
Have we no worth to call our own?
Shall we not vindicate our part,
In the firm breast, and upright heart?
Reader, these virtues may be thine,
Tho' in superior light they shine.
I can't discharge great Hardwick's trust—
True—but my soul may still be just.
And tho' I can't the state defend,
I'll draw the sword to serve my friend.

Two golden Virtues are behind,
Of equal import to the mind;

Prudence,

VISION VI.

Prudence, to point out Wisdom's way,
Or to reclaim us when we stray;
Temp'rance, to guard the youthful heart,
When Vice and Folly throw the dart;
Each Virtue, let the world agree,
Daily resides with you and me.
And when our souls in friendship join,
We'll deem the social bond divine;
Thro' ev'ry scene maintain our trust,
Nor e'er be timid or unjust.
That breast, where Honour builds his throne,
That breast, which Virtue calls her own,
Nor int'rest warps, nor fear appalls,
When danger frowns, or lucre calls.
No! the true friend collected stands,
Fearless his heart, and pure his hands.
Let int'rest plead, let storms arise,
He dares be honest, though he dies.

MARRIAGE,
VISION VII.

Inscribed to Miss ****.

FAIREST, this vision is thy due,
I form'd th' instructive plan for you.
Slight not the rules of thoughtful age,
Your welfare actuates every page;
But ponder well my sacred theme,
And tremble, while you read my dream.

Those awful words, " 'Till death do part,"
May well alarm the youthful heart:
No after-thought when once a wife;
The die is cast, and cast for life;
Yet thousands venture ev'ry day,
As some base passion leads the way.
Pert Silvia talks of wedlock-scenes,
Tho' hardly enter'd on her teens;
Smiles on her whining spark, and hears
The sugar'd speech with raptur'd ears;

Impatient

VISION VII.

Impatient of a parent's rule,
She leaves her fire and weds a fool.
Want enters at the guardlefs door,
And Love is fled, to come no more.

Some few there are of fordid mould,
Who barter youth and bloom for gold;
Carelefs with what, or whom they mate,
Their ruling paffion's all for ftate.
But Hymen, gen'rous, juft, and kind,
Abhors the mercenary mind:
Such rebels groan beneath his rod,
For Hymen's a vindictive god;
Be joylefs ev'ry night, he faid,
And barren be their nuptial bed.

Attend, my fair, to Wifdom's voice,
A better fate fhall crown thy choice.
A married life, to fpeak the beft,
Is all a lottery confeft:
Yet if my fair one will be wife,
I will infure my girl a prize;
Tho' not a prize to match thy worth,
Perhaps thy equal's not on earth.

'Tis

'Tis an important point to know,
There's no perfection here below.
Man's an odd compound, after all,
And ever has been since the Fall.
Say, that he loves you from his soul,
Still man is proud, nor brooks controul,
And tho' a slave in Love's soft school,
In wedlock claims his right to rule.
The best, in short, has faults about him,
If few those faults, you must not flout him.
With some, indeed, you can't dispense,
As want of temper, and of sense.
For when the sun deserts the skies,
And the dull winter evenings rise,
Then for a husband's social pow'r,
To form the calm, conversive hour;
The treasures of thy breast explore,
From that rich mine to draw the ore;
Fondly each gen'rous thought refine,
And give thy native gold to shine;
Shew thee, as really thou art,
Tho' fair, yet fairer still at heart.

Say,

VISION VII.

Say, when life's purple blossoms fade,
As soon they must, thou charming maid;
When in thy cheeks the roses die,
And sickness clouds that brilliant eye;
Say, when or age or pains invade,
And those dear limbs shall call for aid;
If thou art fetter'd to a fool,
Shall not his transient passion cool?
And when thy health and beauty end,
Shall thy weak mate persist a friend?
But to a man of sense, my dear,
Ev'n then thou lovely shalt appear;
He'll share the griefs that wound thy heart,
And weeping claim the larger part;
Tho' age impairs that beauteous face,
He'll prize the pearl beyond its case.

In wedlock when the sexes meet,
Friendship is only then compleat.
" Blest state! where souls each other draw,
" Where love is liberty and law!"
The choicest blessing found below,
That man can wish, or Heaven bestow!

Trust me, these raptures are divine,
For lovely Chloe once was mine!
Nor fear the varnish of my style,
Tho' poet, I'm estrang'd to guile.
Ah me! my faithful lips impart
The genuine language of my heart!

 When bards extol their patrons high,
Perhaps 'tis gold extorts the lie;
Perhaps the poor reward of bread——
But who burns incense to the dead?
He, whom a fond affection draws,
Careless of censure, or applause;
Whose soul is upright and sincere,
With nought to wish, and nought to fear.

 Now to my visionary scheme
Attend, and profit by my dream.

 Amidst the slumbers of the night,
A stately temple 'rose to sight;
And ancient as the human race,
If Nature's purposes you trace.
This fane, by all the wise rever'd,
To Wedlock's pow'rful god was rear'd,

Hard

VISION VII.

Hard by I faw a graceful fage,
His locks were frofted o'er by age;
His garb was plain, his mind ferene,
And wifdom dignified his mien.
With curious fearch his name I fought,
And found 'twas Hymen's fav'rite—Thought.

   Apace the giddy crowds advance,
And a lewd fatyr led the dance:
I griev'd to fee whole thoufands run,
For oh! what thoufands were undone!
The fage, when thefe mad troops he fpy'd,
In pity flew to join their fide:
The difconcerted pairs began
To rail againft him, to a man;
Vow'd they were ftrangers to his name,
Nor knew from whence the dotard came.

   But mark the fequel—for this truth
Highly concerns impetuous youth:
Long ere the honey-moon could wane,
Perdition feiz'd on ev'ry twain;
At ev'ry houfe, and all day long,
Repentance ply'd her fcorpion thong;

                             Difguft

Disgust was there with frowning mien,
And every wayward child of Spleen.

Hymen approach'd his awful fane,
Attended by a num'rous train:
Love with each soft and nameless grace,
Was first in favour and in place:
Then came the god with solemn gait,
Whose ev'ry word was big with fate;
His hand a flaming taper bore,
That sacred symbol, fam'd of yore:
Virtue, adorn'd with ev'ry charm,
Sustain'd the god's incumbent arm;
Beauty improv'd the glowing scene
With all the roses of eighteen:
Youth led the gayly-smiling fair,
His purple pinions wav'd in air:
Wealth, a close hunks, walk'd hobbling nigh,
With vulture-claw, and eagle-eye,
Who threescore years had seen, or more,
('Tis said his coat had seen a score;)
Proud was the wretch, tho' clad in rags,
Presuming much upon his bags.

A female

A female next her arts display'd,
Poets alone can paint the maid:
Trust me, Hogarth, (tho' great thy fame)
'Twould pose thy skill to draw the same;
And yet thy mimic pow'r is more
Than ever painter's was before:
Now she was fair as cygnet's down,
Now as Mat Prior's Emma, brown;
And, changing as the changing flow'r,
Her dress she vary'd ev'ry hour:
'Twas Fancy, child!—You know the fair,
Who pins your gown, and sets your hair.

Lo! the god mounts his throne of state,
And sits the arbiter of fate:
His head with radiant glories drest,
Gently reclin'd on Virtue's breast:
Love took his station on the right,
His quiver beam'd with golden light.
Beauty usurp'd the second place,
Ambitious of distinguish'd grace;
She claim'd this ceremonial joy,
Because related to the boy;

(Said

(Said it was her's to point his dart,
And speed its passage to the heart;)
While on the god's inferior hand
Fancy and Wealth obtain'd their stand.

And now the hallow'd rites proceed,
And now a thousand heart-strings bleed.
I saw a blooming trembling bride,
A toothless lover join'd her side;
Averse she turn'd her weeping face,
And shudder'd at the cold embrace.

But various baits their force impart:
Thus titles lie at Celia's heart:
A passion much too foul to name,
Costs supercilious prudes their fame:
Prudes wed to publicans and sinners;
The hungry poet weds for dinners.

The god with frown indignant view'd
The rabble covetous or lewd;
By ev'ry vice his altars stain'd,
By ev'ry fool his rites profan'd:
When Love complain'd of Wealth aloud,
Affirming Wealth debauch'd the crowd;

Drew

VISION VII.

Drew up in form his heavy charge,
Defiring to be heard at large.
 The god confents; the throng divide,
The young efpous'd the plaintiff's fide:
The old declar'd for the defendant;
For Age is Money's fworn attendant.
 Love faid, that wedlock was defign'd
By gracious Heav'n to match the mind;
To pair the tender and the juft,
And his the delegated truft:
That Wealth had play'd a knavifh part,
And taught the tongue to wrong the heart;
But what avails the faithlefs voice?
The injur'd heart difdains the choice.—
 Wealth ftrait reply'd, that Love was blind,
And talk'd at random of the mind:
That killing eyes, and bleeding hearts,
And all th' artillery of darts,
Were long ago exploded fancies,
And laugh'd at even in romances.
Poets indeed ftyle Love a treat,
Perhaps for want of better meat:

And Love might be delicious fare,
Cou'd we, like poets, live on air.
But grant that angels feast on Love,
(Those purer essences above)
Yet Albion's sons, he understood,
Preferr'd a more substantial food.
Thus while with gibes he dress'd his cause,
His grey admirers hemm'd applause.

With seeming conquest pert and proud,
Wealth shook his sides, and chuckled loud;
When Fortune, to restrain his pride,
And fond to favour Love beside,
Op'ning the miser's tape-ty'd vest,
Disclos'd the Cares which stung his breast:
Wealth stood abash'd at his disgrace,
And a deep crimson flush'd his face.

Love sweetly simper'd at the sight,
His gay adherents laugh'd outright.
The god, tho' grave his temper, smil'd,
For Hymen dearly priz'd the child.
But he who triumphs o'er his brother,
In turn is laugh'd at by another.

VISION VII.

Such cruel scores we often find
Repaid the criminal in kind.
For Poverty, that famish'd fiend!
Ambitious of a wealthy friend,
Advanc'd into the Miser's place,
And star'd the stripling in the face;
Whose lips grew pale, and cold as clay;
I thought the chit would swoon away.

   The god was studious to employ
His cares to aid the vanquish'd boy;
And therefore issu'd his decree,
That the two parties strait agree.
When both obey'd the God's commands,
And Love and Riches join'd their hands.

   What wond'rous change in each was wrought,
Believe me, fair, surpasses thought.
If Love had many charms before,
He now had charms, ten thousand more.
If Wealth had serpents in his breast,
They now were dead, or lull'd to rest.

   Beauty, that vain affected thing,
Who join'd the hymeneal ring,

Approach'd with round unthinking face,
And thus the trifler states her cafe.

 She said, that Love's complaints, 'twas k
Exactly tally'd with her own;
That Wealth had learn'd the felon's arts,
And robb'd her of a thousand hearts;
Desiring judgment against Wealth,
For falsehood, perjury, and stealth:
All which she cou'd on oath depose,
And hop'd the court would slit his nose.

 But Hymen, when he heard her name,
Call'd her an interloping dame;
Look'd thro' the crowd with angry state,
And blam'd the porter at the gate,
For giving entrance to the fair,
When she was no essential there.

 To sink this haughty tyrant's pride,
He order'd Fancy to preside.
Hence, when debates on beauty rise,
And each bright fair disputes the prize,
To Fancy's court we strait apply,
And wait the sentence of her eye;

           In

In Beauty's realms she holds the seals,
And her awards preclude appeals.

L I F E.

V I S I O N VIII.

LET not the young my precepts shun;
Who slight good counsels, are undone.
Your poet sung of Love's delights,
Of halcyon days and joyous nights;
To the gay fancy lovely themes;
And fain I'd hope they're more than dreams.
But, if you please, before we part,
I'd speak a language to your heart.
We'll talk of Life, tho' much, I fear,
Th' ungrateful tale will wound your ear.
You raise your sanguine thoughts too high,
And hardly know the reason why:

But say Life's tree bears golden fruit,
Some canker shall corrode the root;
Some unexpected storm shall rise;
Or scorching suns, or chilling skies;
And (if experienc'd truths avail)
All your autumnal hopes shall fail.

" But, Poet, whence such wide extremes?
" Well may you style your labours Dreams.
" A son of sorrow thou, I ween,
" Whose visions are the brats of Spleen.
" Is bliss a vague unmeaning name—
" Speak then the passions' use or aim;
" Why rage desires without controul,
" And rouse such whirlwinds in the soul;
" Why Hope erects her tow'ring crest,
" And laughs, and riots in the breast?
" Think not, my weaker brain turns round,
" Think not, I tread on fairy ground.
" Think not, your pulse alone beats true—
" Mine makes as healthful music too.

" Our joys, when life's soft spring we trace,
" Put forth their early buds apace.

" See

VISION VIII.

" See the bloom loads the tender shoot,
" The bloom conceals the future fruit.
" Yes, manhood's warm meridian sun
" Shall ripen what in spring begun.
" Thus infant roses, ere they blow,
" In germinating clusters grow;
" And only wait the summer's ray,
" To burst and blossom to the day."
What said the gay unthinking boy?—
Methought Hilario talk'd of joy!
Tell, if thou canst, whence joys arise,
Or what those mighty joys you prize.
You'll find (and trust superior years)
The vale of life a vale of tears.
Could Wisdom teach, where joys abound,
Or riches purchase them, when found,
Would scepter'd Solomon complain,
That all was fleeting, false, and vain?
Yet scepter'd Solomon cou'd say,
Returning clouds obscur'd his day.
Those maxims, which the preacher drew,
The royal sage experienc'd true.

He knew the various ills that wait
Our infant and meridian ſtate;
That toys our earlieſt thoughts engage,
And diff'rent toys maturer age;
That grief at ev'ry ſtage appears,
But diff'rent griefs at diff'rent years;
That vanity is ſeen, in part,
Inſcrib'd on ev'ry human heart;
In the child's breaſt the ſpark began,
Grows with his growth, and glares in man.
But when in life we journey late,
If follies die, do griefs abate?
Ah! what is life at fourſcore years?—
One dark, rough road of ſighs, groans, pains, and
    tears!

  Perhaps you'll think I act the ſame,
As a ſly ſharper plays his game:
You triumph ev'ry deal that's paſt,
He's ſure to triumph at the laſt;
Who often wins ſome thouſands more
Than twice the ſum you won before.

But

VISION VIII.

But I'm a lofer with the reft,
For Life is all a deal at beft;
Where not the prize of wealth or fame,
Repays the trouble of the game;
(A truth no winner e'er deny'd,
An hour before that winner dy'd).
Not that with me thefe prizes fhine,
For neither fame nor wealth are mine.
My cards!—a weak plebeian band,
With fcarce an honour in my hand,
And, fince my trumps are very few,
What have I more to boaft than you!
Nor am I gainer by your fall!
That harlot Fortune bubbles all.

'Tis truth (receive it ill or well)
'Tis melancholy truth I tell.
Why fhould the preacher take your pence,
And fmother truth to flatter fenfe?
I'm fure, phyficians have no merit,
Who kill, thro' lenity of fpirit.

That Life's a game, divines confefs,
This fays at cards, and that at chefs:

But

But if our views be center'd here,
'Tis all a losing game, I fear.

 Sailors, you know, when wars obtain,
And hostile vessels crowd the main,
If they discover from afar
A bark, as distant as a star,
Hold the perspective to their eyes,
To learn its colours, strength, and size;
And when this secret once they know,
Make ready to receive the foe.
Let you and I from sailors learn
Important truths of like concern.

 I clos'd the day, as custom led,
With reading, till the time of bed;
Where Fancy, at the midnight hour,
Again display'd her magic pow'r,
(For know, that Fancy, like a spright,
Prefers the silent scenes of night.)
She lodg'd me in a neighb'ring wood,
No matter where the thicket stood;
The Genius of the place was nigh,
And held two pictures to my eye.

VISION VIII.

The curious painter had pourtray'd
Life in each juſt and genuine ſhade.
They, who have only known its dawn,
May think theſe lines too deeply drawn;
But riper years, I fear, will ſhew,
The wiſer artiſt paints too true.

One piece preſents a rueful wild,
Where not a ſummer's ſun had ſmil'd:
The road with thorns is cover'd wide,
And Grief ſits weeping by the ſide;
Her tears with conſtant tenor flow,
And form a mournful lake below;
Whoſe ſilent waters, dark and deep,
Thro' all the gloomy valley creep.

Paſſions that flatter, or that ſlay,
Are beaſts that fawn, or birds that prey.
Here Vice aſſumes the ſerpent's ſhape;
There Folly perſonates the ape;
Here Av'rice gripes with harpies' claws;
There Malice grins with tygers' jaws;
While ſons of miſchief, Art and Guile,
Are alligators of the Nile.

Ev'n

LIFE.

Ev'n Pleasure acts a treach'rous part,
She charms the sense, but stings the heart;
And when she gulls us of our wealth,
Or that superior pearl, our health,
Restores us nought but pains and woe,
And drowns us in the lake below.

There a commission'd angel stands,
With desolation in his hands!
He sends the all-devouring flame,
And cities hardly boast a name:
Or wings the pestilential blast,
And lo! ten thousands breathe their last:
He speaks—obedient tempests roar,
And guilty nations are no more:
He speaks—the fury Discord raves,
And sweeps whole armies to their graves:
Or Famine lifts her mildew'd hand,
And Hunger howls thro' all the land.

Oh! what a wretch is man, I cry'd,
Expos'd to death on ev'ry side!
And sure as born, to be undone
By evils which he cannot shun!

Besides

VISION VIII.

Besides a thousand baits to sin,
A thousand traitors lodg'd within!
For soon as Vice assaults the heart,
The rebels take the dæmon's part.

I sigh, my aching bosom bleeds;
When strait the milder plan succeeds.
The lake of tears, the dreary shore,
The same as in the piece before.
But gleams of light are here display'd,
To chear the eye and gild the shade.
Affliction speaks a softer style,
And Disappointment wears a smile.
A group of Virtues blossom near,
Their roots improve by ev'ry tear.

Here Patience, gentle maid! is nigh,
To calm the storm, and wipe the eye;
Hope acts the kind physician's part,
And warms the solitary heart;
Religion nobler comfort brings,
Disarms our griefs, or blunts their stings;
Points out the balance on the whole,
And Heav'n rewards the struggling soul.

But

But while thefe raptures I purfue,
The Genius fuddenly withdrew.

DEATH.

VISION the Laſt.

'TIS thought my Viſions are too grave*;
    A proof I'm no deſigning knave.
Perhaps if Int'reſt held the ſcales,
I had devis'd quite diff'rent tales;
Had join'd the laughing low buffoon,
And ſcribbled ſatire and lampoon;
Or ſtirr'd each ſource of ſoft deſire,
And fann'd the coals of wanton fire;
Then had my paltry Viſions ſold,
Yes, all my dreams had turn'd to gold;

* See the Monthly Review of New Books, for February 1751.

Had

VISION IX.

Had prov'd the darlings of the town,
And I—a poet of renown!

Let not my aweful theme surprize,
Let no unmanly fears arise.
I wear no melancholy hue,
No wreaths of cypress or of yew.
The shroud, the coffin, pall, or herse,
Shall ne'er deform my softer verse:
Let me consign the fun'ral plume,
The herald's paint, the sculptur'd tomb,
And all the solemn farce of graves,
To undertakers and their slaves.

You know, that moral writers say
The world's a stage, and life a play;
That in this drama to succeed,
Requires much thought, and toil indeed!
There still remains one labour more,
Perhaps a greater than before.
Indulge the search, and you shall find
The harder task is still behind;
That harder task, to quit the stage
In early youth, or riper age;

To

DEATH.

To leave the company and place,
With firmness, dignity, and grace.

Come, then, the closing scenes survey;
'Tis the last act which crowns the play.
Do well this grand decisive part,
And gain the plaudit of your heart.
Few greatly live in Wisdom's eye—
But oh! how few who greatly die!
Who, when their days approach an end,
Can meet the foe, as friend meets friend.

Instructive heroes! tell us whence
Your noble scorn of flesh and sense!
You part from all we prize so dear,
Nor drop one soft reluctant tear:
Part from those tender joys of life,
The Friend, the Parent, Child, and Wife.
Death's black and stormy gulph you brave,
And ride exulting on the wave;
Deem thrones but trifles all!—no more—
Nor send one wishful look to shore.

For foreign ports and lands unknown,
Thus the firm sailor leaves his own;

Obedient

VISION IX.

Obedient to the rising gale,
Unmoors his bark, and spreads his sail;
Defies the ocean, and the wind,
Nor mourns the joys he leaves behind.

 Is Death a pow'rful monarch? True—
Perhaps you dread the tyrant too!
Fear, like a fog, precludes the light,
Or swells the object to the sight.
Attend my visionary page,
And I'll disarm the tyrant's rage.
Come, let this ghastly form appear,
He's not so terrible when near.
Distance deludes th' unwary eye,
So clouds seem monsters in the sky:
Hold frequent converse with him now,
He'll daily wear a milder brow.
Why is my theme with terror fraught?
Because you shun the frequent thought.
Say, when the captive pard is nigh,
Whence thy pale cheek and frighted eye?
Say, why dismay'd thy manly breast,
When the grim lion shakes his crest?

Because these savage fights are new—
No keeper shudders at the view.
Keepers, accustom'd to the scene,
Approach the dens with look serene,
Fearless their grisly charge explore,
And smile to hear the tyrants roar.

" Ay—but to die! to bid adieu!
" An everlasting farewell too!
" Farewell to ev'ry joy around!
" Oh! the heart sickens at the sound!"

Stay, stripling—thou art poorly taught—
Joy didst thou say?—discard the thought.
Joys are a rich celestial fruit,
And scorn a sublunary root.
What wears the face of joy below,
Is often found but splendid woe.
Joys here, like unsubstantial fame,
Are nothings with a pompous name;
Or else, like comets in the sphere,
Shine with destruction in their rear.

Passions, like clouds, obscure the sight,
Hence mortals seldom judge aright.

The

VISION IX.

The world's a harsh unfruitful soil,
Yet still we hope, and still we toil;
Deceive ourselves with wond'rous art,
And disappointment wrings the heart.

   Thus when a mist collects around,
And hovers o'er a barren ground,
The poor deluded trav'ler spies
Imagin'd trees and structures rise;
But when the shrouded sun is clear,
The desert and the rocks appear.

   " Ah—but when youthful blood runs high,
" Sure 'tis a dreadful thing to die!
" To die! and what exalts the gloom,
" I'm told that man survives the tomb!
" O! can the learned prelate find
" What future scenes await the mind?
" Where wings the soul, dislodg'd from clay?
" Some courteous angel point the way!
" That unknown somewhere in the skies!
" Say, where that unknown somewhere lies;
" And kindly prove, when life is o'er,
" That pains and sorrows are no more.

"For doubtless dying is a curse,
"If present ills be chang'd for worse."
    Hush, my young friend, forego the theme,
And listen to your poet's dream.
    Ere-while I took an evening walk,
Honorio join'd in social talk.
Along the lawns the zephyrs sweep,
Each ruder wind was lull'd asleep.
The sky, all beauteous to behold,
Was streak'd with azure, green, and gold;
But, tho' serenely soft and fair,
Fever hung brooding in the air;
Then settled on Honorio's breast,
Which shudder'd at the fatal guest.
No drugs the kindly wish fulfil,
Disease eludes the doctor's skill.
The poison spreads through all the frame,
Ferments, and kindles into flame.
From side to side Honorio turns,
And now with thirst insatiate burns.
His eyes resign their wonted grace,
Those friendly lamps expire apace!

VISION IX.

The brain's an uselesp organ grown,
And Reason tumbled from his throne.—
  But while the purple surges glow,
The currents thicken as they flow;
The blood in ev'ry distant part
Stagnates and disappoints the heart;
Defrauded of its crimson store,
The vital engine plays no more.
  Honorio dead, the fun'ral bell
Call'd ev'ry friend to bid farewell.
I join'd the melancholy bier,
And dropp'd the unavailing tear.
  The clock struck twelve—when nature sought
Repose from all the pangs of thought;
And while my limbs were sunk to rest,
A vision sooth'd my troubled breast.
  I dream'd the spectre Death appear'd,
I dream'd his hollow voice I heard!
Methought th' imperial tyrant wore
A state no prince assum'd before.
All nature fetch'd a gen'ral groan,
And lay expiring round his throne.

I gaz'd—

I gaz'd—when ſtrait aroſe to ſight
The moſt deteſted fiend of night.
He ſhuffled with unequal pace,
And conſcious ſhame deform'd his face.
With jealous leer he ſquinted round,
Or fix'd his eyes upon the ground.
From hell this frightful monſter came,
Sin was his ſire, and Guilt his name.

 This fury, with officious care,
Waited around the Sov'reign's chair;
In robes of terrors dreſt the king,
And arm'd him with a baneful ſting;
Gave fierceneſs to the tyrant's eye,
And hung the ſword upon his thigh.
Diſeaſes next, a hideous crowd!
Proclaim'd their maſter's empire loud;
And, all obedient to his will,
Flew in commiſſion'd troops to kill.

 A riſing whirlwind ſhakes the poles,
And lightning glares, and thunder rolls.
The Monarch and his train prepare
To range the foul tempeſtuous air.

Strait to his shoulders he applies
Two pinions of enormous size !
Methought I saw the ghastly form
Stretch his black wings, and mount the storm.
When Fancy's airy horse I strode,
And join'd the army on the road.
As the grim conqu'ror urg'd his way,
He scatter'd terror and dismay.
Thousands a pensive aspect wore,
Thousands who sneer'd at Death before.
Life's records rise on ev'ry side,
And Conscience spreads those volumes wide;
Which faithful registers were brought
By pale-ey'd Fear and busy Thought.
Those faults which artful men conceal,
Stand here engrav'd with pen of steel,
By Conscience, that impartial scribe !
Whose honest palm disdains a bribe.
Their actions all like critics view,
And all like faithful critics too.
As guilt had stain'd life's various stage,
What tears of blood bedew'd the page !

All shudder'd at the black account,
And scarce believ'd the vast amount!
All vow'd a sudden change of heart,
Would Death relent, and sheathe his dart.
But, when the awful foe withdrew,
All to their follies fled anew.

 So when a wolf, who scours at large,
Springs on the shepherd's fleecy charge,
The flock in wild disorder fly,
And cast behind a frequent eye;
But, when the victim's borne away,
They rush to pasture and to play.
 Indulge my dream, and let my pen
Paint those unmeaning creatures, Men.

 Carus, with pains and sickness worn,
Chides the slow night, and sighs for morn;
Soon as he views the eastern ray,
He mourns the quick return of day;
Hourly laments protracted breath,
And courts the healing hand of Death.

 Verres, oppress'd with guilt and shame,
Shipwreck'd in fortune, health, and fame,

VISION IX.

Pines for his dark sepulchral bed,
To mingle with th' unheeded dead.

With fourscoure years grey Natho bends,
A burden to himself and friends;
And with impatience seems to wait
The friendly hand of ling'ring fate.
So hirelings with their labour done,
And often eye the western sun.

The monarch hears their various grief,
Descends, and brings the wish'd relief.
On Death with wild surprize they star'd;
All seem'd averse! All unprepar'd!

As torrents sweep with rapid force,
The grave's pale chief pursu'd his course.
No human pow'r can or withstand,
Or shun the conquests of his hand.
Oh! could the prince of upright mind,
And, as a guardian angel, kind,
With ev'ry heart-felt worth beside,
Turn the keen shaft of Death aside,
When would the brave Augustus join
The ashes of his sacred line?

But

But Death maintains no partial war,
He mocks a sultan or a czar.
He lays his iron hand on all——
Yes, kings, and sons of kings, must fall!
A truth Britannia lately felt,
And trembled to her center!——*

    Cou'd ablest statesmen ward the blow,
Wou'd Granville own this common foe?
For greater talents ne'er were known
To grace the fav'rite of a throne.

    Cou'd genius save—wit, learning, fire—
Tell me, would Chesterfield expire?
Say, wou'd his glorious sun decline,
And set like your pale star or mine?

    Cou'd ev'ry virtue of the sky—
Wou'd Herring †, Butler ‡, Secker § die?
Why this address to peerage all—
Untitled Allen's virtues call!

* Referring to the death of his late Royal Highness Frederick Prince of Wales.
† Archbishop of Canterbury.
‡ Late Bishop of Durham.
§ Bishop of Oxford.

VISION IX.

If Allen's worth demands a place,
Lords, with your leave, 'tis no difgrace.
Tho' high your ranks in heralds' rolls,
Know Virtue too ennobles fouls.
By her that private man's renown'd,
Who pours a thoufand bleffings round;
While Allen takes Affliction's part,
And draws out all his gen'rous heart;
Anxious to feize the fleeting day,
Left unimprov'd it fteal away;
While thus he walks with jealous ftrife
Thro' goodnefs, as he walks thro' life,
Shall not I mark his radiant path?—
Rife, mufe, and fing the Man of Bath!
Publifh abroad, cou'd goodnefs fave,
Allen wou'd difappoint the grave;
Tranflated to the heav'nly fhore,
Like Enoch, when his walk was o'er.

Not Beauty's pow'rful pleas reftrain—
Her pleas are trifling, weak, and vain;
For women pierce with fhrieks the air,
Smite their bare breafts, and rend their hair.

All

DEATH.

All have a doleful tale to tell,
How friends, sons, daughters, husbands fell!
   Alas! is life our fav'rite theme!
'Tis all a vain, or painful dream.
A dream which fools or cowards prize,
But slighted by the brave or wise.
Who lives, for others' ills must groan,
Or bleed for sorrows of his own;
Must journey on with weeping eye,
Then pant, sink, agonize, and die.

   And shall a man arraign the skies,
Because man lives, and mourns, and dies?
Impatient reptile! Reason cry'd;
Arraign thy passion and thy pride.
Retire, and commune with thy heart,
Ask, whence thou cam'st, and what thou art.
Explore thy body and thy mind,
Thy station too, why here assign'd.
The search shall teach thee life to prize,
And make thee grateful, good, and wise.
Why do you roam to foreign climes,
To study nations, modes, and times;

A science

VISION IX.

A science often dearly bought,
And often what avails you nought?
Go, man, and act a wiser part,
Study the science of your heart.
This home philosophy, you know,
Was priz'd some thousand years ago *.
Then why abroad a frequent guest?
Why such a stranger to your breast?
Why turn so many volumes o'er,
Till Dodsley can supply no more?
Not all the volumes on thy shelf,
Are worth that single volume, Self.
For who this sacred book declines,
Howe'er in other arts he shines;
Tho' smit with Pindar's noble rage,
Or vers'd in Tully's manly page;
Tho' deeply read in Plato's school;
With all his knowledge is a fool.

Proclaim the truth—say, what is man?
His body from the dust began;

* KNOW THYSELF—a celebrated saying of Chilo, one of the seven wise men of Greece.

And

DEATH.

And when a few short years are o'er,
The crumbling fabric is no more.
  But whence the soul? From heav'n it came!
Oh! prize this intellectual flame.
This nobler Self with rapture scan,
'Tis mind alone which makes the man.
Trust me, there's not a joy on earth,
But from the soul derives its birth.
Ask the young rake (he'll answer right)
Who treats by day, and drinks by night,
What makes his entertainments shine,
What gives the relish to his wine;
He'll tell thee, (if he scorns the beast)
That social pleasures form the feast.
The charms of beauty too shall cloy,
Unless the soul exalts the joy.
The mind must animate the face,
Or cold and tasteless ev'ry grace.
  What! must the soul her pow'rs dispense
To raise and swell the joys of sense?—
Know too, the joys of sense controul,
And clog the motions of the soul;

Forbid

VISION IX.

Forbid her pinions to aspire,
Damp and impair her native fire:
And sure as Sense (that tyrant!) reigns,
She holds the empress, Soul, in chains.
Inglorious bondage to the mind,
Heaven-born, sublime, and unconfin'd!
She's independent, fair, and great,
And justly claims a large estate;
She asks no borrow'd aids to shine,
She boasts within a golden mine;
But, like the treasures of Peru,
Her wealth lies deep, and far from view.
Say, shall the man who knows her worth,
Debase her dignity and birth;
Or e'er repine at Heaven's decree,
Who kindly gave her leave to be;
Call'd her from nothing into day,
And built her tenement of clay?
Hear and accept me for your guide,
(Reason shall ne'er desert your side.)
Who listens to my wiser voice,
Can't but applaud his Maker's choice;

Pleas'd

Pleas'd with that First and Sov'reign Cause,
Pleas'd with unerring Wisdom's laws;
Secure, since Sov'reign Goodness reigns;
Secure, since Sov'reign Pow'r obtains.

With curious eyes review thy frame,
This science shall direct thy claim.
Dost thou indulge a double view,
A long, long life, and happy too?
Perhaps a farther boon you crave—
To lie down easy in the grave?
Know then my dictates must prevail,
Or surely each fond wish shall fail.—

Come then, is Happiness thy aim?
Let mental joys be all thy game.
Repeat the search, and mend your pace,
The capture shall reward the chace.
Let ev'ry minute, as it springs,
Convey fresh knowledge on its wings;
Let ev'ry minute, as it flies,
Record thee good as well as wise.
While such pursuits your thoughts engage,
In a few years you'll live an age.

Who

VISION IX.

Who measures life by rolling years?
Fools measure by revolving spheres.
Go thou, and fetch th' unerring rule
From Virtue's, and from Wisdom's school.
Who well improves life's shortest day,
Will scarce regret its setting ray;
Contented with his share of light,
Nor fear nor wish th' approach of night.
And when Disease assaults the heart,
When Sickness triumphs over Art,
Reflections on a life well past,
Shall prove a cordial to the last;
This med'cine shall the soul sustain,
And soften or suspend her pain;
Shall break Death's fell tyrannic pow'r,
And calm the troubled dying hour.

   Blest rules of cool prudential age!
I listen'd, and rever'd the sage.
When lo! a form divinely bright
Descends and bursts upon my sight,

A Seraph

DEATH.

A Seraph of illustrious birth!
(Religion was her name on earth)
Supremely sweet her radiant face,
And blooming with celestial grace!
Three shining cherubs form'd her train,
Wav'd their light wings, and reach'd the plain;
Faith, with sublime and piercing eye,
And pinions flutt'ring for the sky;
Here Hope, that smiling angel, stands,
And golden anchors grace her hands;
There Charity, in robes of white,
Fairest and fav'rite maid of light!

 The seraph spake—'tis Reason's part,
To govern, and to guard the heart;
To lull the wayward soul to rest,
When hopes and fears distract the breast.

Reason may calm this doubtful strife,
And steer thy bark thro' various life:
But when the storms of death are nigh,
And midnight darkness veils the sky,

Shall

VISION IX.

Shall Reason then direct thy sail,
Disperse the clouds, or sink the gale?
Stranger, this skill alone is mine,
Skill! that transcends his scanty line.

That hoary sage has counsel'd right—
Be wise, nor scorn his friendly light.
Revere thyself—thou'rt near ally'd
To angels on thy better side.
How various e'er their ranks or kinds,
Angels are but unbodied minds;
When the partition-walls decay,
Men emerge angels from their clay.

Yes, when the frailer body dies,
The soul asserts her kindred skies.
But minds, tho' sprung from heav'nly race,
Must first be tutor'd for the place.
(The joys above are understood,
And relish'd only by the good)
Who shall assume this guardian care?
Who shall secure their birthright there?

Souls are my charge—to me 'tis giv'n
To train them for their native heav'n.

 Know then—Who bow the early knee,
And give the willing heart to me;
Who wisely, when Temptation waits,
Elude her frauds, and spurn her baits;
Who dare to own my injur'd cause,
(Tho' fools deride my sacred laws;)
Or scorn to deviate to the wrong,
Tho' Persecution lifts her thong;
Tho' all the sons of hell conspire
To raise the stake, and light the fire;
Know, that for such superior souls,
There lies a bliss beyond the poles;
Where spirits shine with purer ray,
And brighten to meridian day;
Where Love, where boundless Friendship rules,
(No friends that change, no love that cools!)
Where rising floods of knowledge roll,
And pour and pour upon the soul!

VISION IX.

But where's the paffage to the fkies?—
The road thro' Death's black valley lies.
Nay, do not fhudder at my tale—
Tho' dark the fhades, yet fafe the vale.
This path the beft of men have trod;
And who'd decline the road to God?
Oh! 'tis a glorious boon to die!
This favour can't be priz'd too high.

 While thus fhe fpake, my looks exprefs'd
The raptures kindling in my breaft:
My foul a fix'd attention gave;
When the ftern Monarch of the Grave
With haughty ftrides approach'd—Amaz'd
I ftood, and trembled as I gaz'd.
The Seraph calm'd each anxious fear,
And kindly wip'd the falling tear;
Then haften'd with expanded wing
To meet the pale terrific King.
But now what milder fcenes arife!
The Tyrant drops his hoftile guife.

He

He ſeems a youth divinely fair,
In graceful ringlets waves his hair.
His wings their whitening plumes diſplay,
His burniſh'd plumes reflect the day.
Light flows his ſhining azure veſt,
And all the angel ſtands confeſt.

 I view'd the change with ſweet ſurprize,
And oh! I panted for the ſkies;
Thank'd Heav'n, that e'er I drew my breath,
And triumph'd in the thoughts of Death.

END OF THE FIRST VOLUME.

www.ingramcontent.com/pod-product-compliance
Lightning Source LLC
Chambersburg PA
CBHW021402230426
43666CB00006B/610